SELF-DISCIPLINE & MENTAL TOUGHNESS

DISCOVER HOW HIGH PERFORMERS ACHIEVE THEIR GOALS
THROUGH SELF-DISCIPLINE AND MENTAL TOUGHNESS

WILLIAM ANDERSON

CONTENTS

THE POWER OF SELF-DISCIPLINE

THE POWER OF MENTAL TOUGHNESS

INTRODUCTION

I have not always been a highly disciplined person. I lacked the self-control to stick to a routine when it came to diet or exercise.

I grew up in Romania, an ex-communist country. The revolution took place in 1989 and I was born in 1996 into a country that was already poor. My parents could afford very little while caring for six children on my father's salary. I always dreamed big and wanted to dedicate my life to something meaningful. I wanted to play professional soccer in Europe, but since we didn't have money to send me to a city where I could join a team to fulfill my goal, I was forced to let this dream go.

At age 18, I saw a fitness influencer, who was so dedicated to his elite fitness. I was inspired to become a fitness influencer as well. I said goodbye to Romania and moved to several countries throughout Europe to chase my dreams, all while working up to 12 hours a day. At the same time, I was working out early in the morning, waking up at 3 AM. You can imagine that waking up so early isn't always a sweet thing to do. Looking back, I can tell that self-discipline was one of my best friends. I made all these sacrifices to obtain the PRO CARD in the Men's Physique Division. After several injuries and my body giving up despite my drive, I went back to Romania and, with much hard work, began a business that eventually made a profit.

This success, through all my failures and getting back up, made me realize that my true path led me to write this book to encourage others to never give up on making something meaningful of their goals, of their lives.

Having realized what discipline is and how to use it to improve my life, I want now to pass on what I have learned to you.

Are you someone who wants more out of life? Have you also come to the conclusion that motivation is hard and you cannot count on it? Are you also not sure how to accomplish what you desire? Then, you have come to the right place. You need the core principles that will help you along the way, and this book can offer you that. It will provide you with insights on how to have self-discipline as well as how high performers think and the habits that they have. Furthermore, you will also discover the importance of delayed gratification, the power of focus, the necessity of having an accountability partner, the benefit of visualization, the value of believing in yourself, and more.

In this book, you will also learn how to develop long-term and consistent self-discipline. The goal here is to help you move beyond simply wanting to do better to setting specific goals and achieving them with self-discipline. I also would like to inspire you to act decisively in any activity you decide to pursue.

Why do you need to have consistent self-discipline? There are actually some benefits that you can gain from it, such as having better self-control, understanding the value of time, being more aware of things, having much better judgments, and so forth. Having consistent self-discipline is worth the effort once you can experience all of its benefits. Otherwise, you will only become average and fail to reach your goals for success in life. In addition to learning about the tips to assist you in developing self-discipline, this book will also cover the different ways to have better mental strength. If you struggle to keep moving forward in the face of challenges or if you believe you lack the drive to continue when motivation begins to decline and discomfort sets in, consistent self-discipline is something that you should practice.

Now that you have learned what this book has to offer, it is time for you to get off that couch and start taking action. You should not wait until you have the motivation to do so. This is the first step you can take to achieve consistent self-discipline. Once you can do this, everything else is easy to follow. While you read through this journey to Self-Discipline, use a pencil to make notes or highlight key components that you want to revisit later. If you like to keep your book free of markings use sticky notes or fold the corners of the pages to find notable points later on. If you have the eBook grab a pad or paper and make key notes as you go along.

The power of self-discipline is a journey that begins now. Are you ready? Let's get going!

1

MAKING THINGS AS SIMPLE AS POSSIBLE

"Discipline is doing what you hate to do, but doing it like you love it."- Cus D'Amato

WHAT EXACTLY IS SELF-DISCIPLINE?

Self-discipline is the capability to move forward, , and act despite any physical or mental discomfort (Sasson, 2022). Self-discipline is also generally understood to be conscious control that is directed toward achieving effective results by removing barriers or obstacles (Zimmerman & Kitsantas, 2014). We reveal it when we knowingly opt to work toward wanting to better ourselves in the face of difficult situations like

13

interruptions, challenges, or unfavorable circumstances. Self-discipline is not the same as willpower or self-motivation. Motivation and willpower can lead to it, as well as perseverance, the capacity to carry out our intentions, and also hard work.

For instance, Jane gets up early every morning to work out. She performs very well at her workplace, putting high-value projects first and avoiding distractions in the process. She takes an online class in the evening and receives her master's degree in about a year. This does not seem possible for most people to accomplish. How is it that people like Jane consistently do so much while having the same hours as everyone else? And how will we be able to boast such achievements in both our personal and professional lives like her? The key to this is self-discipline. It is what makes us carry out our great intentions and ambitions, despite our reluctance and unwillingness to take action. If we possess self-discipline, we will be able to postpone momentary pleasure or put up with temporary hardship or discomfort in order to pursue long-term gain in the future.

Self-discipline prevents you from overeating chips or other junk food after deciding to eat healthier meals, or it can prevent you from spending your entire income on useless stuff that you do not need. Every individual has a distinct definition of self-discipline; some of us may find it easier than others to exercise control. Everybody, however, may learn to develop their self-discipline muscles (Parincu, 2022).

Due to the false perception that it is something difficult and that it needs a lot of effort and commitment to get, the term "self-discipline" sometimes elicits some discomfort and reluctance from some people (Parincu, 2022). In reality, developing self-discipline and practicing it can be enjoyable, take little effort, and have significant advantages. As opposed to what some people believe, true self-discipline is not a harsh or strict way of life, and it does not have anything to do with being narrow-minded or having little intellect. This ability is a manifestation of inner courage and perseverance, two qualities that are essential for managing daily activities and accomplishing success.

In the end, we should make self-discipline our best friend. Why? Because we can rely on it as the root of all the good qualities that we dream to possess and the path that will lead us to success, despite all the obstacles on the way.

WHAT ARE THE BENEFITS OF SELF-DISCIPLINE?

Throughout our lives, it is necessary for us to learn and hone the talent of self-discipline since it will benefit us greatly in our lives. There will inevitably be tasks we do not enjoy doing and times when we are distracted from our goals. For this reason, it is crucial to cultivate self-discipline so that we can strive even during these periods of lower motivation. What other benefits does self-discipline have? Here are some of them.

CONTROLLING YOUR EMOTIONS BETTER

Abiding by the morally upright course of action is a small but essential part of discipline. It also becomes one technique for mastering and gaining control over our emotions. With self-discipline, we will be able to keep our worries, hesitations, and all the negativity we have in our heads at bay when faced with a challenging or stressful situation. For example, when doing a team project at work, perhaps you are grouped with a coworker who never does things the right way. You may feel frustrated with them and tempted to get angry instead of trying to teach them how to do things the correct way. In this scenario, you will get exhausted and overwhelmed if you let your emotions take over you. Doing so would be one of the main causes of failure in the many obstacles that life throws our way. Instead of courting failure and then whining about it, we should work on developing self-discipline.

REALIZING THE VALUE OF TIME

Time is a precious resource that waits for no one. Our entire lives, we have been hearing this saying from our elders, whether it was at school or at home. However, did we actually follow it? Each action we take needs to have a timetable. Deciding to adhere to a schedule or, more often than not, deadlines will teach us the value of time in our lives. Eventually, life will be better and more organized when we are disciplined.

HAVING BETTER JUDGMENTS

Decision-making is one of the most powerful abilities that we, humans, have been given, with profound implications for our lives, and not only. Thus, we can either make a wise decision and choose to live today and tomorrow better, or we can choose badly and fall into a deep pit hole. We can better distinguish between what is good and what violates the laws of nature and society when we have self-discipline. For example, when we realize that we are really intoxicated, we can decide whether to take a taxi or drive ourselves home. That one decision has the potential to change everything.

MAKING YOU BECOME MORE ACTIVE

We will begin to understand that life is not about sitting around waiting for a chance to knock at your door if we practice self-discipline. Our minds gradually come to the realization that sitting around and moping will not help us in the long run. At that point, we start acting and taking control of our lives. In turn, as we let go of the laziness that had been preventing us for so long from taking a step toward our desire, we will be able to become a better and improved version of ourselves.

BECOMING MORE SELF-AWARE

When we develop the ability to be self-disciplined, we learn more about ourselves and our capabilities. We have the opportunity to recognize our strengths and shortcomings as well as work on them according to our needs and circumstances. That makes it possible for us to get rid of the personality traits that have prevented us from succeeding in life. After a while, we will be able to stop relying on our friends or even our families to judge us more positively. We will become our own best critics.

GROWING INTO YOUR BEST SELF

Only when we deserve it does success come to us. With our present personalities, we may not be able to become successful in life. We must therefore make changes day after day and strive to be our best selves. We can constantly better ourselves through self-discipline. When we regularly practice something, we get better and better each day. Thus, self-discipline is essential for achievement and personal development in life.

IMPROVING YOUR PERFORMANCE

If we want to improve in our careers, it is absolutely essential that we are driven and fully committed to our work regardless of how large or pointless the task appears to be. We need commitment anywhere, whether we are hosting a friend's birthday party or giving a presentation. Both on a professional and a personal level, taking things lightly can turn out to be very disastrous. Of course, no host wants to hear negative comments about the party they have organized. Also, no one would want to give a bad presentation and get humiliated in front of the audience as this can be very shameful. In all areas of our lives, we must be dedicated and motivated. That is one of the major points supporting the value of discipline since it teaches us how to perform better.

IMPROVING YOUR PERSONAL RELATIONSHIPS

Tom decided to procrastinate working on his project during the week because he felt lazy and unmotivated to do so. When the weekend arrived, he realized that he needed to finish the project by the next Monday. Instead of using his weekend off for spending time with his wife and kids, he had to work on completing the project. In this case, Tom did not practice self-discipline when he actually needed to. When we have self-discipline, we always finish our work on time. There is a ton of time available to us. Because of this, we will be able to have all the available time to bond with our loved ones. We can use our time without worrying about unfinished business. A time spent together without guilt—this is a result of having a strong self-discipline. In the end, all of our personal relationships will be improved significantly.

IS DISCIPLINE SOMETHING YOU INHERIT?

Discipline comes from inside of us. Interestingly, it does not really matter if we come from a family that consistently exercises discipline because it is neither contagious nor inherited. We must develop discipline ourselves; it cannot come from outside of us. For instance, the majority of us have encountered people who have come from dysfunctional families, unfortunate life situations, and every imaginable terrible circumstance, yet these people are disciplined.

We do not get discipline from our families. Some people are very disciplined and were born into dysfunctional families; others are not very self-disciplined and were born into very good families. As an example, people from problematic family circumstances typically follow one of two ways. They either let themselves dwell on their pain and, sadly, never reach their full potential, or they embrace their struggles to motivate them to rise above their difficulties and improve themselves for the better. Which direction they take is entirely up to each of them to decide. They simply need the strength of character to avoid repeating the mistakes that made their family lives hard once they are adults and have separated from their families. We can decide to act differently if we recognize the areas where our parents failed. For instance, a parent who has a gambling addiction that causes their entire family agony can teach their kids the behavior they need to avoid to stop the cycle.

This indicates that nobody can point the finger at someone else for their lack of discipline. We have no right to hold our friends, parents, or even our schools accountable for our own lack of control. We must own up to it. We need to be able to motivate ourselves. Nobody else can give us the self-discipline, emotional restraint, and control we need to succeed in our lives. Every person must choose for themselves, understanding that effective discipline is quite difficult, particularly when first starting.

IS DISCIPLINE YOUR CHOICE TO MAKE?

Nobody just gets up from their sleep one day and declares that they have mastered the art of self-discipline so suddenly. Similar to a muscle, discipline needs to be developed over time. Have you tried to train your self-discipline today? Perhaps your answer to this is no. However, you might have already made a few choices this morning that would make you say yes to the question. The issue here is that we frequently pay more attention to the aspects of life where discipline is lacking than to those where it is developed well.

People who are excellent at exercising self-discipline do so frequently because they consistently take the appropriate actions to tackle the problem at hand. It means that discipline is a choice that we decide to take in order to overcome the challenges we have to face. Over time, maintaining a particular behavior becomes a habit. For instance, even though you enjoy sleeping, you only sleep a maximum of six hours per night. You value your love for your family and your ability to contribute at work more than sleep. You simply care for other aspects of your life more than sleep, not because you dislike sleep any less. In this scenario, you choose to prioritize your loved ones, your job, and your family over getting more sleep.

We will be able to sustain our efforts and take the steps required for achievement by choosing to adopt discipline in our lives. Without self-discipline, we are bound to act hastily and recklessly. We can put ourselves in check by leading a disciplined life, and it is entirely our decision to choose whether we want to have self-discipline or not.

KEY TAKEAWAYS

- As explained above, self-discipline is the capability to move forward, maintain motivation, and act despite any physical or mental discomfort. It is the path we must take in order to accomplish success.
- It also has a lot of advantages for us such as controlling our emotions better, realizing the value of time, having better judgments, making us more active, becoming more aware, supporting us to become the best version of ourselves, improving our performance, and making our personal relationships better.
- Discipline is also not something that we inherit from other people because it comes from within ourselves.

2

HOW TO INSTILL A DESIRE FOR CONSISTENT SELF-DISCIPLINE

"You don't get discipline from an external source. You have to get it from you."- Jocko Willink

The key to being able to lead others and also ourselves is discipline. Focus and self-control lead to contentment, happiness, and success. When we exercise self-control and discipline, we can achieve more of the goals that are most important to us. Self-discipline is the bridge between setting goals and realizing them. However, it is not that easy to get the desire to actually have consistent self-discipline in our lives. How do we do this? What are the steps we can take to accomplish it?

ENVISIONING THE FUTURE

IMAGINING YOUR IDEAL SELF

The first step to getting the desire for self-discipline is to imagine what your ideal self would be. This is the best and highest version of yourself that you can think of. With this in mind, consider the following questions:

- Who do you hope to become?
- What do you hope to do, encounter, and possess?
- What kind of life do you desire to have in the future?

- What contributions, whether small or significant, do you intend to make to the world?
- What type of work will suit your ideal self?
- What kind of life would you lead if you succeeded in becoming your ideal self? What drives your desire to adopt this identity? Why do you choose it?

Write your responses to these questions. When you are through, you will have clearly defined your ideal self. You now have something to work toward. A lot of us are scared of what our ideal selves are like because we fear that we will never be able to become them. However, if we refuse to imagine and think of it, how would we ever accomplish it? We need to envision the best version of ourselves before we can take all the other necessary steps to reach that point.

WRITING DOWN AND VISUALIZING THE ACTIONS AND BEHAVIORS ATTACHED TO THIS IDEAL VERSION OF YOURSELF

What habits must you form in order to live up to your ideal self and potential? What actions will you take to accomplish that? What behaviors do you need to adopt for that? Here are some of the forms that discipline may take:

- Health and fitness: Perhaps you can make a timetable to work out at the gym three times a week and follow through with the schedule as best as you are able to.
- Mental and intellectual: You can decide to read one book a week or write down a short story or poem when you have time on the weekends in order to train your intellect and brain.
- Social and emotional: You may choose to spend more quality time with your family or partner by planning a weekly date night or family dinner at a restaurant to bond more with them.

- Spiritual and religious: You can make a schedule to meditate for 15 minutes every day or go to church every week in order to deepen your spirituality.

When we can visualize all these types of discipline that we wish to apply in our lives, it will be much easier for us to do them. If we know what is waiting for us in the future, we will feel more inspired and motivated to start taking action to have consistent self-discipline.

THINKING ABOUT THE END RESULTS

Developing a vision of the outcomes and hanging onto it is key to the self-discipline battle. One little, wise choice keeps self-discipline in place when we are presented with a challenge that slows us down or completely breaks us away from the path. Instead of surrendering to temptation and the pressure of the present, we need to be able to think forward. We can overcome the challenge by learning to say no to the temptations that come our way. When we can envision the end results of self-discipline that are possible, we will be able to apply it in our lives more easily and with fewer struggles.

RECOGNIZING THE REASONS FOR LACK OF DISCIPLINE

There are several things that influence our success. All kinds of abilities, habits, and mindsets play a big role in our own achievements. Although there are other important factors, self-discipline stands out among the rest. When we lack self-discipline, we might lead a lifestyle that is unhealthy.

Our capacity for self-discipline is one of the most important factors in determining our level of success in life. Its effects can be observed in a variety of life aspects. It bears repeating: If we desire to achieve our goals and live a happy life, we need to have consistent self-discipline. Yet a lot of us often lack this. Why does this happen? What are the reasons?

MISUNDERSTANDING THE BASIC CONCEPT

Many people struggle with self-discipline mostly because they misunderstand what this concept implies. From their perspective, self-discipline is something uncomfortable and obsessive. They wished that discipline was easy and fun to do. Because of this, whenever these people attempt to become more disciplined, it ends up being a struggle that does not feel fair to them. Because they do not like it, they quickly go back to their usual habits.

BEING LAZY

If we have a hard time practicing self-discipline, it may be because we lack inner strength and are too lazy. In this case, we avoid engaging in things that need persistence and effort. It is in our human nature that we prefer peaceful, enjoyable behaviors to demanding tasks that need a lot of effort. In contrast to self-discipline, laziness is comfortable and not complicated. It is much easier to sit around and live in our comfort zone instead of taking action to apply self-discipline in our lives. A lot of us fall into this and have a lack of discipline.

FALLING INTO LIFE TEMPTATIONS

Almost all of us are very vulnerable to many temptations day after day. Social media and TV advertising constantly scream at us to buy their products. Supermarkets and shopping centers offer a wide range of goods for sale. We also have access to a number of entertainment options, from social media, TV shows, and movies to nice restaurants, music concerts, and many other distractions in this modern world. They all seem so impossible to escape from. How can we refuse to browse through social media that offers a pleasant escape from everyday life or avoid the beautifully displayed and tempting items in the store? Self-discipline is bound to be lacking if all of these pleasures are accepted and followed carelessly and without using common sense.

BEING SCARED TO FAIL

We all fear something. Another reason for a lack of self-discipline is when we have a fear of failure. This speaks to a deficiency of inner strength, suppressing initiative and determination. Oftentimes accepting failure results in losing control. When people can accept the potential of failing, it will be challenging to maintain self-discipline. Before something even happens, those who have a fear of failure will be pessimistic from the start, and they might even decide to not take action at all, fearing the end results.

UNDERSTANDING THE CONSEQUENCES OF LACK OF DISCIPLINE

Everybody can recall a period when they procrastinated in moving toward their goals. We desire to eat healthier, yet we find it impossible to give up the sweet treats we enjoy. Despite our intention to get out of bed sooner, we often stay up late, until after one in the morning. We all have been there before. If we continue to practice the one negative habit that prevents us from mastering the main habit that will ultimately lead to our achievements, we will feel terrible.

In the same way that discipline has its advantages, it can also have negative consequences. As an example, we may frequently find ourselves hitting the snooze button after knowing that we have made the commitment to get up at 6 a.m. in the morning. The negative consequence of this is that we would not get things done, and we would end up getting angry at ourselves for not being further ahead on a specific task that we wished to have completed by a certain time. In addition to getting angry, there are several more consequences of our lack of discipline that we should be aware of.

PREVENTING YOU FROM ACCOMPLISHING YOUR GOALS

Distractions can also increase in this area. If we are not careful, accepting even little distractions because of our own excuses will keep us frustrated and pull us further away from our goals and purpose. When we do not wish to do something, many of us will create different excuses so that we can avoid doing it. After that, we will regret it. We would ask ourselves why we do not get things done and become irritated because we have not seen the progress we hope to make.

LOWERING YOUR SELF-ESTEEM

In your mind, this may seem stupid, but give it some thought. Because you lack something or you have someone that you are envious of, you experience poor self-esteem or insecurity. When we see how easy it is for certain people to work or run their businesses, and they are making a lot of money, while we are still trying to be stable enough, it will make us feel like we should just quit what we are doing since we are nowhere close to where we need to be. Our self-esteem level will decrease when we do not have self-discipline because our progress is hindered by our own inaction.

TAKING AWAY YOUR FOCUS

A messy surrounding leads to a cluttered mind, which will take away our focus from our tasks. If everything around us is disorganized, then our thoughts will also be disorganized. When our spaces are not arranged well, we will not be able to take action to transform ourselves. We need to have a strategy for this, and self-discipline will keep us moving forward with our intended course of action. If we cannot practice self-discipline, we will stray away from our focus and not follow through with our plans.

SHOWING THAT YOU LACK SELF-RESPECT

When we are not sure or do not know how to do something, we will give up on it. We neglect the fact that we are also making the decision to break our commitment. We all enjoy being lazy and not doing anything, but we do not like it when we are disrespected. This kind of lack of discipline is dangerous because when we decide to abandon a task, we disrespect ourselves and our own commitment.

MAKING YOU PROCRASTINATE MORE

If we lack self-discipline, laziness will cause us to put things off more. We will not be able to accomplish our goals if we do this. When we do not know how to control ourselves and fall into temptations, we will procrastinate on our tasks and produce poor-quality work in the end.

KEY TAKEAWAYS

- Before we can start on our journey to have consistent self-discipline, we need to first find the desire and willpower to begin it.
- In order to discover this desire, we have to imagine our ideal selves, write down and visualize the actions and behaviors attached to the ideal version of ourselves, and what kind of outcomes will come our way from having consistent self-discipline.
- We also need to realize that there are reasons that can cause us to have a lack of discipline, such as having a misunderstanding of the basic concept, being lazy or lacking inner power, falling into life temptations, and being scared to fail.
- If we fail to improve our self-discipline, there are consequences that we must face. It will prevent us from achieving our goals, lower our self-esteem, take away our focus, show that we do not have respect for ourselves, and make us procrastinate more.
- Once we realize all of the above, we will be able to see how important it is to have self-discipline and that we need to start applying it consistently in our lives so that we can stay on the path to success.

3

GOAL-SETTING AND SELF-DISCIPLINE

"When you have a goal, when you have a vision, everything becomes easy."- Arnold Schwarzenegger

O f all the factors that influence someone's success and happiness, only one ensures long-term, sustained success in all areas of life, and that is self-discipline. For instance, developing self-discipline can be difficult, but it will be well worth the effort in the field of health and fitness. Many of us may feel insecure about how our bodies look after eating so much junk food all the time. We want to lose weight in order to feel better, look better, and wear all the clothes we want. In order to achieve this, we need to set specific goals, such as planning to go to the gym three times a week or starting a healthy meal plan by cooking homemade food. As a result of being disciplined in this area, we will develop a better, healthier lifestyle and become more confident about how we look. That is why we need to set goals before we can have consistent self-discipline. Those who do not have a clear and specific goal in life will find it more challenging to maintain discipline since they are still not sure what they desire to achieve. By contrast, we are far more inclined to possess the willpower to chase our goals if we have a certain purpose that we wish to see come true in the future.

WHY SHOULD YOU SET SPECIFIC GOALS?

Do you have any personal goals? What are your plans for the upcoming year? What do you want out of life? Creating goals is the very first step in achieving them. It represents the beginning of our achievements. It occurs when we start actively shaping our lives rather than just passively existing for no reason at all. We must establish our precise goals in order to help us develop consistent self-discipline. If we do not have specific goals, we may not be able to have self-discipline because we are not sure what we want to achieve from it. Before we learn about the steps in setting goals, let us consider the advantages we can get from them.

HAVING MORE CONTROL OF YOUR LIFE

These days, a lot of people are living their lives as if they are sleeping. Despite their best efforts, they do not feel as though they are making progress toward their goals. This is a result of their lack of direction over their goals and where they wish to go in the future. Adults who have worked for years are surprised when they approach their 30s or 40s, and students are unsure of what to do next after graduating from college (Celes, 2022). Without setting goals, we might end up spending our entire lives bouncing up and down without accomplishing anything. We are really just achieving other people's objectives, not our own. We will begin living a life that we have intentionally created when we take the time to set goals and consider our ambitions and aspirations. We should actively take charge and consider what we want for ourselves as opposed to having others tell us what to do and which direction to take.

ACQUIRING MAXIMUM RESULTS

All accomplished people, professional athletes, and top performers set their own goals. We all have heard of Mark Zuckerberg, a self-taught computer programmer as well as the co-founder, chairman, and CEO of Meta (META), previously recognized as Facebook. He is known for creating the social networking site in his dormitory at Harvard University in 2004, while it was still called Facemash, along with some of his friends (Downey, 2019). Before deciding to create the site, he had set goals and even gone on to make it in his dorm room. Although not having all the fancy facilities, Zuckerberg was able to realize his goal because of how disciplined he was.

When we set goals, we have something to aim for. Instead of sitting back and waiting for everything to happen by itself, we need to make sure that we are challenging ourselves to achieve the best results. We also need to realize that there is also room for improvement. How will things go better if we do not set clear goals and benchmarks? There is essentially nothing to work toward, and although we might be devoting a lot of effort, it may not be effective. When we decide to set goals, we are shooting for the moon. We take action more than we otherwise would because of the goals we set.

What do you hope to achieve in a year? How about in three years? Setting goals forces us to prepare ahead, which allows us to develop an action plan. Even if things do not go exactly as we had planned, it is still okay because we can review, modify our plans, and then guide our lives in the direction of our goals slowly but surely.

GIVING YOU CLEAR FOCUS

By setting goals, we will be able to become more focused. Our goals offer us a clear focus on what to concentrate our time and energy on, whereas our life purpose provides us with a general direction. Let's imagine that you have decided to start a bakery. Even though you do not know how to make it happen, just establishing a goal provides you with something to focus on. As you come up with ideas, you realize that you may begin this goal by researching the brands and local bakery market. You will try to understand people's preferences for desserts and bread. After that, you can enroll in baking classes to develop your abilities. You may then test recipes and serve your products to friends before selling them at the same time. We can think of the outcomes as the output and our energy as the input. When we have a goal, we establish a focus point in which we are able to direct our energy to gain the maximum benefit.

CREATING ACCOUNTABILITY

Setting goals will make us become accountable. Instead of only talking, we are now obligated to take action. This accountability is one that you have to yourself and not to everyone else. Nobody knows and is aware of all the goals we set. Even when we succeed in reaching our goals, others have nothing to benefit from it. By having clear goals, we can know if we are on track, and if not, we will be able to determine how to solve them.

As an example, if you want to establish your own personal blog, you need to set goals, like finishing a specific number of posts per week, reaching a target traffic goal each week, and acquiring a particular number of clients each month. This will make you accountable for achieving these goals. You will then need to keep an eye on your progress weekly while working on your plan. You also have to make the appropriate adjustments if you ever realize you are falling short.

LIVING YOUR BEST LIFE

Goals also guarantee that we get the most out of life. Time will go by in our lives whether we like it or not. We will be a year older in a year. We will be ten years older in ten years. Setting goals with clear deadlines and measurements helps us make the most of our time here in this world. Our goals will enable us to maximize our life purpose if we have already found it.

Let's imagine the world as our oyster. There are countless possibilities for activities, adventures, and interactions with people that we can have. There are endless opportunities for what we are able to achieve. What if you had complete freedom? What would you like to see, do, and encounter in life? We must set our goals, work toward them, and observe them as we build our lives for the better.

HOW DO YOU SET YOUR GOALS?

Setting goals is a useful strategy for developing consistent self-discipline. We can choose how to use our time and resources to achieve maximum outcomes by setting goals and establishing a clear plan for how we will get to our desired targets. Without goals, it might be challenging to plan how to advance toward becoming self-disciplined and having a successful life. How do we set goals then? Here are some ways we can use it.

VISUALIZING YOUR GOALS AND EXPERIENCING THEM

If our goal is to spend more time with our family by not working nights and weekends, we must experience the goal by visualizing it or by really doing it right away. This will strengthen our self-discipline as we proceed through the necessary measures to accomplish the goal. It is also crucial to keep ourselves healthy physically, mentally, emotionally, as well as spiritually. It takes more than simply having enough money to avoid working outside the home to be able to spend more time with our family. We also need to be physically healthy, capable of handling stress, and willing to invest time in our own personal growth.

PLANNING AHEAD

Some external influences will always present a challenge to our daily routines. Making strategies for the best, worst, and most likely scenarios will help us keep our routines. For example, we can go on a vacation in order to find situations that can challenge our self-discipline (Ali, 2021). Self-disciplined people will use their vacation time and actively build flexibility into their daily schedule instead of sticking to a strict schedule that will never work. When returning to a normal schedule, it is much easier to make adjustments because they already know what needs to change.

UNDERSTANDING YOUR WHY

This is possibly the most important technique for developing strong self-discipline. We can concentrate better on the bigger picture if we are aware of why we want to accomplish a certain goal. Knowing why we desire to lose weight, such as to reduce our chance of developing diabetes and its complications, will increase our likelihood of success. Simply wishing to lose weight because we think we would be healthier at a lighter weight is far less likely to be successful. We can take it a step further by considering how diabetes affects not just us but also our family and the whole population. It is much more challenging to run a marathon just to reach the finish line than it is to run a marathon in support of a purpose or charity that is precious to our hearts.

SETTING SMART GOALS

SMART is an abbreviation that stands for specific, measurable, achievable, relevant, and time-based (Herrity, 2022). Every component of the SMART system functions in harmony to provide a goal that is thoroughly planned out, identifiable, and trackable. A lot of us may have previously set goals that were challenging to accomplish because they were framed incorrectly, excessively, or insufficiently. A badly constructed goal might make achieving it seem overwhelming and impossible. These issues can be resolved by setting SMART goals. Whether we are making goals for our personal or professional lives, employing the SMART goal structure may give us a strong framework for success.

- Specific: We need to be as detailed and precise as we can about what we wish to accomplish. We will discover the actions required to attain our goals more thoroughly the more specific our goals are (Herrity, 2022). We can say, for example, "I want to get a job managing an HR team for a startup company."
- Measurable: What concrete evidence will demonstrate that we are moving closer to our goal? If our goal is to manage an HR team for a startup company, for instance, we can measure our progress by the number of HR roles we have applied for or the number of interviews we have had.

Setting checkpoints along the journey will allow us to assess our progress and make necessary adjustments. When we reach these checkpoints, we need to remember to reward ourselves in a small yet meaningful way.

- Achievable: Have you established achievable goals? We will be able to stay motivated and focused if we set goals we can practically achieve within a set period of time. Using the above case of getting a job managing an HR team, we should be aware of the qualifications, experience, and abilities required to obtain that position. We have to consider whether we can attain a goal now or whether we need to take more preparation steps to be properly ready before we start working toward it (Herrity, 2022).

- Relevant: We need to think about if our goals are relevant when setting them. Our goals should all be consistent with our values and longer-term objectives. We may want to reconsider a goal if it does not help us achieve our broader ambitions. We should question why the objective is significant to us, how reaching it will benefit us, and how it will advance our long-term objectives.

- Time-based: What time frame do you have in mind for your goal? A deadline can help motivate us and assist us with prioritizing. For instance, we can allow ourselves six months if our goal is to obtain a promotion to a higher-ranking senior position. By then, if we have not succeeded in our goal, give it some thought and consider the reason why. It is possible that our goal was unachievable, our schedule was too tight, or we encountered unforeseen obstacles.

KEY TAKEAWAYS

- Consistent self-discipline starts with goal-setting. If we do not have a specific goal, with precise or clear reasons for wanting to attain that goal, the likelihood of us being disciplined will be very low.
- Setting goals will give you a clear focus and more control over your life, and encourage you to be more accountable, while also allowing you to get maximum results and envision your best life.
- Setting SMART goals goes hand in hand with visualizing, planning, and understanding the reasons for them. To achieve our goal, we need to establish a plan and, no matter what obstacles stand in our way, we have to remain dedicated to doing whatever is necessary to accomplish it.

4

DOING SOMETHING THAT SUCKS EVERYDAY

"Do something that sucks every single day of your life. That's how you grow."- David Goggins

Why should we do something that sucks? This is a challenge that encourages us to recognize and build on our abilities, even as we recognize our limits. It concentrates and capitalizes on our biggest potential, which lies in our top strengths and skills. However, to make that potential a reality and thus perform at our best requires self-discipline.

Everything worth accomplishing needs sacrifice at the start. Confidence is developed through success, and in order to succeed, we must do things that suck, are difficult, and are uncomfortable. Even when we think that we have finished a task, we are actually just 40% done (Davy, 2019). The Navy SEALs refer to this as the 40% rule, which was made popular by David Goggins, who competed in 14 track races totaling more than 100 miles each while spending most of his time serving on active duty and with a possibly deadly heart condition that only allowed him to function with around 75% of his heart's capacity (Firsich, 2020).

David Goggins encouraged us to ignore our strengths and concentrate on our shortcomings because they challenge and unsettle us, and we should get used to feeling uncomfortable. Real improvement comes from a willingness to experience discomfort by confronting our inner monsters, fears, and negative emotions. Once we embrace the challenge, though, how do we go about doing things that suck and are uncomfortable?

FACING THINGS THAT SUCK

How frequently did you have a challenging task to complete? And how often have you simply avoided dealing with it? We have all come across this situation. When we deal with it and get it done, it usually is not as horrible as we initially feared. The truth is, we only need to face it first, and everything will become easier. For example, James has been wanting to resume his fitness routine. He usually likes to run, lift weights, do yoga, and practice martial arts. Anything further is an additional advantage for him. The challenge here is integrating it into his family life. He had to accept the idea that in order to run and lift weights, he would need to wake up early and make it a priority. He, therefore, has developed this habit for over four weeks. When his alarm goes off at 5:30 a.m., he starts getting ready for his run. We all know that running so early in the morning sucks; it still annoys James even after four whole weeks.

But there is another way to look at what sucks, and that is to see it as a character-building activity. No matter how hard it is in the beginning, we feel good afterward. It feels amazing to do something that we do not look forward to or are unsure we can complete. Additionally, it raises the bar for what we believe we are capable of. Thus, by starting the day with an activity that we dread, everything else that day will be a little bit easier. Pushing through one challenging situation puts the upcoming ones into perspective. We develop tolerance to things that suck. Moreover, it cultivates strength, persistence, and a fighting spirit.

For instance, your supervisor criticizes you, you then have a horrible argument with your coworker at work, and you make an error in your big daily tasks. These will still be annoying and upsetting. However, when you have already overcome a challenge that morning, they do not have as big of a negative impact on you anymore.

GETTING YOURSELF READY

If we decide to do something that sucks, we will encounter internal resistance initially. We can, however, take action to lessen the resistance. If we want to run at 6 a.m. each morning, the time and

45

run do not change. However, there are other things we are able to change. If we plan to run, we need to do certain things to prepare for the night beforehand. Perhaps we can lay out our freshly washed shorts, shirts, and socks and put them on the couch. We can also prepare our jogging clothes and sneakers and put them in a place that we can view. We may also place our headphones and smartphones on the table next to our clothing.

Moreover, if we find it hard to change in the bedroom because we are afraid to wake up our partner, we can go out of the room, turn on the bathroom light, and get dressed there instead. As we have prepared our headphones for the run, we can put on music that will be able to motivate us. Because we have found the motivation and gotten relaxed, it is then easier for us to stretch and walk prior to beginning the run. All these preparations are the things that we can do in order to run early in the morning even though it is very difficult.

UNDERSTANDING THE EXPOSURE THEORY

Using the example above, we want to start waking up early to run and get a good fitness routine. We need to keep in mind that we plan to get up at 6 a.m. in the morning. We have to know that we will not break any world record on our first day of doing that. We should give our bodies time to warm up and get used to it. This is where our minds get in the zone. As time goes by, we can then start to put in more effort and increase the challenge as well as intensity. The idea behind this also drives exposure therapy.

When something or someone makes people uncomfortable or afraid, they are more likely to avoid it. Therapists implement the concept of exposure therapy to help patients in overcoming their fears and anxieties by breaking down the cycle of avoidance and anxiety (Yetman, 2021). It works out by presenting someone with a fear-inducing stimulus in a safe setting. A person with social anxiety, for instance, might avoid coming to events or busy places.

In order to make the patient feel at ease in these kinds of social situations, a therapist will expose the patient to them in exposure therapy. They must learn to be comfortable with any level of stimulation they need to handle (Yetman, 2021).

As another example, the majority of people's greatest fear is public speaking. In order to face this by using exposure theory, we can get a person to talk face-to-face with another person. Then, we can encourage them to talk to two people at once. Afterward, we can ask them to speak to three people. They can continue doing this until 100 people are in the room. By increasing the stimulus, we also increase our capacity for dealing with it. We greatly enhance resilience in this case.

We can do this too with anything that sucks. We can start off slowly and gradually increase our effort and stimulus as time passes. After that, we will see that we have transformed ourselves. We learn how to handle situations that really suck, including things that we previously never thought of doing or completing.

KEY TAKEAWAYS

- When we do something that sucks, we will change. We will develop previously lacking confidence, persistence, and thus self-discipline.
- If we plan to do things that suck, we need to do them first thing in the morning. Afterward, everything will become easier to do.
- Once we can overcome things that suck, we will never forget the feeling of strength, accomplishment, and satisfaction.
- When we do things that suck, we can begin slowly and then steadily increase our effort and intensity. After that, we will be able to significantly increase our adaptability and see how much we can change.

5

CHANGING WHAT YOU CAN CHANGE AND LETTING GO OF WHAT YOU CANNOT CHANGE

"If you can't control it, let it go."- Gary R. McClain

When something does not go our way, it is quite easy to start thinking of the wrong things. We stray into areas and thoughts over which we have no control. We begin to dwell on all the negative aspects of our situation and worry about all the negative outcomes that might occur. We lose sight of our role in determining our reality, which clouds our judgment. We make an effort to remain optimistic and efficient on good days. On bad days, we drown in worry over imagining what the future will hold. We picture it, then begin to experience it, leaving us feeling powerless and afraid. When we focus on what we cannot change, we stop doing things we are supposed to do to become disciplined in order to reach success.

The key is to channel our efforts into the things we can control, letting go of the rest. By doing so, we can increase our resilience and begin to make progress regardless of the level of chaos going on around us. Attempting to control everything in life is a losing battle. Despite our best efforts, focusing on things whose outcomes we cannot actually change is a waste of energy. The first step to this is to recognize what we can and cannot control.

HOW DO YOU FEEL MORE IN CONTROL?

Focusing on what we can change about ourselves or our surroundings and trying to move in the right direction will help us feel more in control. We will be able to greatly improve our quality of life if we take charge of everything within our power and let go of the rest. The first step in empowering ourselves is recognizing what we can and cannot control and then redirecting our energy to those things. We can fully accept responsibility for our lives in this manner, without adding to our stress levels in the process. It all begins with us; an aspect of leading a self-disciplined and healthy life entails taking complete accountability for our actions and what we are able to control in our lives.

So how do we regain control of the things that are within our reach? The answer lies in practicing mindfulness, which involves being attentive, self-aware, and involved in what we are doing and where we are at that present (Bastos, 2020). When we practice mindfulness, we develop the attentional skill of 'seeing' our thoughts and feelings and changing how we respond to them (Christian, 2021). We can gradually teach ourselves to focus on the here and now in order to be more aware of our thoughts and reactions to the environment around us.

In order to have better self-discipline, we need the transformational power of mindfulness that is accessible to everyone. Here are some methods to help us begin our journey toward getting control over what we can control.

PAYING CLOSE ATTENTION TO YOUR FEELINGS AND EMOTIONS

We are encouraged to get rid of the notion that we have any control over our feelings and emotions through the practice of mindfulness. Alternatively, it encourages us to pay more attention to what we are feeling and thus understand it better. We can better control the influence that emotions have on our behavior by becoming aware of the ups and downs of our own thoughts. In this sense, mindfulness is a method of control. As we become more conscious of our emotions and how we react to them, we will understand that the voices in our heads are not always to be trusted. Getting control over how feelings and emotions might affect our behavior requires acknowledging that occasionally our thoughts are not helpful and they do not have to be the ones that should determine what we do.

CONCENTRATING ON THE PRESENT

We are able to access mindfulness at any time and from any place. An important technique for developing a mindful state is to keep our focus on the present moment. Since tranquility and peace of mind are much more likely to be found in the present, it is important to keep our minds in there. That is also the place where our focus is strongest and in which we can be far more in tune with our feelings, thoughts, and physical sensations (Bastos, 2020). In contrast, when our attention is on another point in time, emotions and feelings that are still present in the past or the future might not only cause us to get distracted, but they can also develop as disorders like anxiety and depression.

When our focus and attention are on the present, we are not preoccupied with what may have been or the things that might happen later. That is, we view our feelings and emotions as temporary instead of permanent. We can refocus our attention when we realize that we are becoming bogged down in negative feelings and emotions by being mindful of the present. This allows us to take charge and be in control of how our emotions affect us.

TAKING ACTION TO CREATE CHANGE

It takes practice to become aware of our emotions and feelings as well as to teach our minds to concentrate on the present. However, the more we do it, the better we will get, and the outcome can significantly affect our well-being in a positive way. We can start doing this by setting some achievable goals. A great approach to getting motivated to take action and make great changes is to think about where we wish our lives to go and the kind of person we desire to become in the future.

WHAT ARE THE THINGS YOU CAN CONTROL IN LIFE?

The main idea of this chapter is to concentrate on the things we can control in order to have consistent self-discipline, but before that, we need to know what those things are first. Here are a few aspects of our lives that we have control over. We will be amazed by the improvements that can develop over time when we can make small progress in these aspects.

HOW YOU COMMUNICATE WITH YOUR LOVED ONES

Although they are not always simple and easy, relationships are the basis of a pleasant and healthy life. Even though we have no control over the actions of our loved ones, we do have power over how we act in a relationship. Healthy communication is where it all begins. Words frequently fall short when trying to convey abstract feelings and thinking processes. In this case, we can use an assertive communication style, which is fantastic news. Developing an assertive communication style can help us get our point across, prevent misunderstandings, and gain a deeper understanding of how our loved ones are feeling (Christian, 2021).

In a relationship, the only one we are able to control is ourselves. If we want to communicate in a healthy way with our loved ones, the following are some examples of an assertive communication style:

- Making direct eye contact. This demonstrates the speaker's self-confidence
- Having an assertive posture that strikes the balance between seriousness and casualness. For instance, rigid posture may be interpreted as hostile, while slouching may be interpreted as weak (Lonczak, 2020).
- Showing the right facial expressions. For the proper message to be sent, expressions that are calm and relaxed are necessary to use.

- Using the right tone of voice. A strong voice indicates assertiveness, whereas raising your voice displays and will probably invite hostility.

HOW YOU MAINTAIN YOUR MENTAL HEALTH

Mental and physical wellness are equally important. Our quality of life is greatly influenced by how actively we take care of our psychological, emotional, and social well-being. Interacting with others, getting sufficient sleep, exercising regularly, and seeking professional assistance when necessary are all ways to maintain good mental health. If life seems out of control, it is extremely crucial to take care of our mental health. When our minds are healthy, and we stay away from bad thoughts, it will be much easier for us to do all the things we need to do. We will not miss all the important things in life when we keep our mental health in check at all times.

HOW YOU RESPOND WHEN SOMETHING NEGATIVE HAPPENS

Our ability to make decisions is at its worst when powerful emotions like fear, rage, or envy take control. It is very easy to lose control and act rashly in this kind of situation. Learning to manage our reactions entails learning to regulate our emotions. By moving from a position of reaction to a place of response, we can do just that. Reacting is defined as acting hastily and unconsciously in response to our feelings. Responding entails pausing to consider what we are thinking or feeling. Prior to engaging in a disagreement or making a choice based on fear, we must ask for the time and space that we require to understand the situation. We can return to the issue once we have calmed down in a more fresh, problem-solving state of mind.

WHAT YOU DO WITH YOUR FREE TIME

We can choose how we use our spare time even though we cannot always control how much of it we have. Our lives can be significantly affected by how we spend our free time. Here are a handful of the activities successful people engage in during their free time, as reported by Inc (Demers, 2022):

- Reading helps us learn new concepts, expand our vocabulary, and preserve our cognitive function.
- Taking courses strengthens our portfolio and makes us more attractive to employers.
- Volunteering helps us gain perspective on life, contribute to our local community, and find our purpose in this world.
- Networking opens up different prospects for both our personal and professional lives.
- Working out can benefit both our physical and mental health.
- Spending quality time with our loved ones fosters connection and creates a network of support.
- Hobbies help us stay creative and mentally active.

WHAT KIND OF NEWS YOU WATCH

A balanced diet is about more than just providing our bodies with healthy foods. It also extends to those things intended for our intellectual consumption, or even for mere entertainment. Our mental well-being is harmed by excessive exposure to negative social media or news reports (Davey, 2020). Although we have no control over the crises that arise in the world, we do have power over how much news we consume, the kinds of programs we watch, and the books we choose to read. We need to take a rest from social media and the news and reflect on how information impacts us and our well-being. In order to put everything into perspective, we have to mix up our information intake with positive news, such as inspiring stories and new inventions that can motivate us.

WHAT TYPE OF MINDSET YOU HAVE

Our chances of success are significantly influenced by our own mindset. We have the ability to transform the restrictive thinking that is stopping us from improving. Dr. Carol Dweck, a psychologist at Stanford University, introduced the idea of fixed and growth mindsets through her studies on how humans handle problems and challenges (Abdou, 2022).

- Fixed mindset: If someone has a fixed mindset, they think that some traits, such as talent and intelligence, are innate and permanent. They typically believe that they will never be good at anything if they are not good at it now.
- Growth mindset: If someone has a growth mindset, they will believe that intelligence and talent can always be improved through practice and hard work.

It should come as no surprise that our mindset greatly affects our ambition, persistence, and success. It is also obvious that adopting a growth mindset can help us become disciplined in our work because we will always try to improve ourselves. We have no control over our circumstances, but we do have power over our mentality. We should strive to cultivate a growth-oriented mindset since we can achieve our goals and face problems by working hard and keeping an open mind.

REALIZING WHEN TO LOOK FOR HELP

Humans are social beings, and supporting one another helps us succeed. We should never isolate ourselves or drive people away if we are experiencing overwhelming and uncontrollable feelings. Rather, admit that we need support and help from others. Then, we should take action to obtain it. We will overcome obstacles and achieve our goals more quickly if we have a support system. For example, if we have a major project at work that we will not be able to finish by ourselves, we have to get assistance from our coworkers so that we can avoid burnout. We can also get inspiration from a mentor or professional coach if we ever need help making a hard decision. In order to keep a positive attitude and make wise judgments as we go through life, it can be helpful to seek out inspirational people to guide us.

KEY TAKEAWAYS

- Attempting to control everything in life is a losing battle. Don't waste your energy on things you cannot change any more. You will get stuck and become stagnant if you try to force control over things that are out of your reach.
- However, there are some parts of life that we can take control of, such as how we communicate with our loved ones, how we maintain our mental health, how we respond when something negative happens, what we do with our free time, what kind of news we watch, what type of mindset we have, and when to look for help.
- If we gain control of what is in our power, we will be able to significantly improve the quality of our lives.
- Furthermore, in order to take charge of the aspects we are able to control, we can pay close attention to our feelings and emotions, concentrate on the present by trying to practice mindfulness, and take action to create change.

6

TAKING RESPONSIBILITY FOR EVERYTHING THAT HAPPENS IN YOUR LIFE, WHETHER GOOD OR BAD

"The moment you take responsibility for everything in your life, is the moment you can change anything in your life."- Hal Elrod

WHY DO YOU NEED TO TAKE RESPONSIBILITY FOR YOUR LIFE?

Our lives are entirely our responsibility. We must acknowledge this if we plan to have consistent self-discipline and accomplish success in our lives and careers. A lot of people believe that everything and everyone else is to blame. For example, in the workplace, where people are connected so intricately and each project has a chain of internal clients who are dependent on one another, it is very easy to come up with excuses for why a problem is not their responsibility. Failure is never the outcome of the decisions they took; each failure has a scapegoat that they may use to avoid taking accountability for their own conduct (Heathfield, 2020).

What happens when we refuse to take responsibility? We are more inclined to view our lives as a failure if we do not take ownership of our own actions because we let the wind blow us around and then blame it for how things played out. We create an unhappy life—one that does not satisfy any of our hopes and expectations—when we fail to appropriately guide our paths and achievements.

Moreover, when we avoid responsibility for the things that happen in our lives, we risk causing other issues, such as pessimistic thoughts, a victimized mindset, constant disagreements, hesitation, stagnancy, and codependency. When we take responsibility, more favorable outcomes are bound to come our way. We have to be careful about the choices and decisions we make if we aspire to a higher quality of life that makes us happy and successful.

Are you driven by a fierce passion? Or do you have a mediocre lens through which you see your reality? Whatever improvements we desire, we have to first assume responsibility for our lives and never completely entrust anyone else with them. When we put our lives in the hands of others, we give others the authority and permission to guide our lives in whatever way they see fit, often at the cost of our own improvement. We do not wish this to happen to us, which is why it is important to start taking responsibility for our own lives.

While taking full responsibility entails holding ourselves completely accountable, it does not imply being alone and living a secluded life separated from other people. It's okay if we accept assistance from others even as we accept full responsibility for our own lives. We can ask for their opinions or that they hold us accountable. Strong social ties play a significant role in helping to create long-lasting happiness for a lot of people. Rather than assuming that other people will understand our needs or wait for them to change, we must also take responsibility for our relationships.

HOW DO YOU TAKE RESPONSIBILITY?

PRIORITIZING YOURSELF

We must first believe that we are deserving of a great life in order to make smarter decisions and take responsibility for our lives. Due to self-limiting beliefs, many people fear taking responsibility. As a result, these people can think that they do not deserve better. We need to keep in mind that occasionally being selfish is not wrong. If we are not giving ourselves love and support, how can we expect others to do the same?

We can prioritize ourselves by engaging in self-love and self-care practices. Loving ourselves can boost our confidence and helps us realize that we have the final say in how we desire our lives to go. A ten-minute meditation, journaling, a warm bath, gardening, and repeating uplifting mantras each day are instances of self-love and self-care practices. To give another example, on the weekends, we can take ourselves to go shopping or go to a spa to reward ourselves for our hard work during the weekdays.

NOT PLACING BLAME ON OTHERS

Stopping the blame game is the first step in taking responsibility for our lives. Why? Because if you do not accept responsibility for your life, you are probably blaming other people or circumstances for your problems. It is always anything other than yourself that is to blame, whether it is a dysfunctional relationship, a difficult childhood, financial difficulties, or other challenges that inevitably happen with life. It is true that life can be unfair. Some people are more unlucky than others. In some situations, you may also be the victim. Even so, what exactly does blaming others accomplish? Playing the victim card? Justification for the unpleasant circumstances of life?

Blaming actually only leads to anger, frustration, and helplessness. The people you point the finger at are usually unaware of your feelings or do not even care. The truth is that while such emotions and feelings may be valid, they will never advance our success or happiness. Getting rid of the blame does not excuse others' unfair conduct. It also does not disregard the challenges of life. However, what we have to know is that our lives are about us and not them. In order to regain the freedom and power that are rightfully ours, we must stop the blame game.

BEING WARY OF EXCUSES

People that are irresponsible frequently find or create a variety of excuses for their actions. An irresponsible individual who desires to make healthier choices might claim that they are unable to do so because they do not have the time. The thing is they could find the time to do it if only they were responsible. There are countless reasons for not making life changes. However, when we let them stop us from changing anything, that reason turns into an excuse.

Trying to make excuses prevents us from having the chance to grow from our mistakes. There is no room for growth when there is no personal responsibility. Without ever moving ahead, we will be trapped in the same place whining and obsessing over the negative things. We will be able to put an end to negativity when we take responsibility for our lives and refrain from making excuses. We will come to the realization that external circumstances are meaningless and our actions are the only thing that truly matters.

REMOVING TOXIC PEOPLE

Genuinely loving and caring people will hold us accountable because they wish to see us succeed in life. Toxic people may wish to prevent us from achieving our goals in order to keep us dependent on them. In this scenario, these people are not our true friends, so we need to remove them from our lives.

We must be responsible for the people we choose to surround ourselves with if we want to take responsibility for our lives. People who frequently criticize, self-loathe, speak poorly of themselves, and complain about our success are not good for our improvement. These people will hinder our progress. We should only maintain interactions that are constructive and healthy. Furthermore, we should work to achieve emotional independence so that we can make better decisions objectively and draw genuine people into our lives.

FOCUSING ON TAKING ACTION

Everybody has their own goals and dreams, but without taking any action, they will never be realized. What good is it to talk about doing something but never follow through? It is impossible to accept responsibility without any action that follows. Our lives will get better even if we just take baby steps in the right direction. We should never forget that our habits are where the action begins. As time passes by, taking small steps every day adds up to a huge step in the end.

LOVING YOURSELF

If we have trouble taking responsibility for ourselves and our actions, it is probably because we do not value ourselves either. Why is this? Because those with very low self-esteem typically do not take responsibility. Rather, the responsibility and blame are placed on others, which fosters a victim mentality. We will not be able to improve our self-esteem until we recognize that we have made mistakes and take responsibility for them. Being responsible gives us the ability to take initiative to better ourselves and other people around us.

If we depend on outside reinforcement in order to boost our self-esteem, such as getting compliments from other people, it means that we give away the power to them. Instead, we should work on developing internal stability. We must know how to value ourselves and who we are as people. When we can love ourselves, there is no other choice but to take responsibility for our lives. Since it is our own reality, the best way to enhance it is for us to take responsibility for our behavior.

GETTING RID OF NEGATIVE SELF-TALK

In order to start taking responsibility, we need to eliminate negative self-talk. Negative self-talk may originate from childhood trauma brought on by abuse in the home or being bullied at school (Murphy, 2021). For instance, if you are body shamed and insulted by bullies as a child, eventually you will start to believe them, which makes you feel horrible and insecure about yourself. These negative, self-restricting beliefs we have about ourselves are frequently the result of projections and judgments made by others (Murphy, 2021). These statements have a tendency to be internalized while we are younger, and as a result, they stick with us as we grow older. It will take some time to break such ingrained negative self-perceptions. However, it is achievable through engaging in self-love and self-care practices.

ACKNOWLEDGING NEGATIVE EMOTIONS

A lot of people find it difficult to accept this. Everyone wants to feel happy and have positive emotions, after all. However, we also need to be responsible for our emotions if we are going to start taking responsibility for ourselves. The fact is that nobody can always be positive and upbeat. Everybody has a dark side in them. The darker side of life will hit us harder in the future if we always ignore or repress it. It is important to be honest about who we are deep inside because we will never improve or be successful in life if we always try to be someone that we are not. In order to be self-disciplined, we need to take responsibility for ourselves no matter the cost.

CULTIVATING COMPASSION FOR YOURSELF

Since we know that we are able to choose the course that our lives can take, taking full responsibility can be challenging. After knowing this fact, some of us may become a little harsh on ourselves. Unfortunately, a lot of us are our own worst critics. We disturb our inner balance when we are being critical of ourselves, and the discouragement that we experience as a result can also make us feel depressed and hopeless about our situations. In order to resolve the issue, we need to cultivate self-compassion. We should try to say positive things to (or about) ourselves and see the humor in the circumstances. By the same token, we should feel thankful for having learned the lesson rather than feeling guilty or resentful. We can discover the wisdom in what we have learned about ourselves instead of feeling like we have wasted our time. When we take responsibility for our lives, even a simple change in perspective can have a significant impact.

NOT INTERNALIZING JUDGMENT

Everybody always has their own opinion about things. However, we should not internalize the judgments that other people have about us. Each of us has our own stance on happiness and success that makes us unique. Even though a lot of our loved ones have the best intentions, they often try to project their own wishes onto us. For instance, some parents may insist that their children choose a particular major in college, career path, or even partner in marriage. We cannot live our lives in order to please others. We are all responsible for living our own lives.

Rather than internalizing the opinions and judgments of others, we should put more effort into getting to know who we are. What do success and happiness seem like in our eyes? What criteria do we use to find a love partner? We have better, more fulfilling lives when we are honest about who we are as people. We must therefore be absolutely honest with ourselves if we want to succeed. It may even be necessary for us to spend some time away from those who are continuously forcing their opinions on us because this can lead to internal conflict and make decision-making extremely difficult.

TAKING RESPONSIBILITY EVEN IF IT IS NOT YOUR FAULT

The more you decide to take responsibility for your life, the more control you will have over it. The first thing to do in order to resolve our problems in life is to take responsibility for them. Due to the misconception that accepting responsibility for our problems also involves accepting fault, many people are reluctant to do so. In our culture, responsibility, and fault frequently go hand in hand. However, they are distinct from one another. For example, if you hit someone with your car, you are both at fault and most certainly have a legal obligation to compensate them. Although hitting that person was not intentional, you would still be the one responsible for it. In this society, fault works out that way. We are responsible for making things right whenever we make a mistake, and that is also how it ought to be.

However, there are also other issues that are not our fault but for which we still bear responsibility. For instance, if you have a business and you are the boss of your company, you will have employees working for you. When someone makes a mistake, let's say an error that causes your company to lose over 1 million dollars, you are the one who has hired that employee. In this case, you will be 100% responsible for that 1-million-dollar mistake, and not that employee. If you had been more careful about who you decided to hire, the company would probably have never lost that money. You accept the consequences that would happen when you chose to hire someone.

As another example, perhaps one day the town you live in is left without electricity, and you are not able to do the things you usually do. Who do you think is responsible for that? Of course, you are. You decided to live in that town and also chose not to buy a generator for your house. Once you accept this fact, you can either move to a different city or get yourself a generator.

All the time, we bear responsibility for things that are not our fault, and this is a fact that we must accept. Fault is in the past and responsibility is in the present. Fault comes from decisions that have previously been made. However, responsibility comes from decisions that we are making every single day.

There is a distinction between holding somebody else responsible for our circumstances and simply blaming them. We alone are responsible for our situations in life. Our misery may be caused by different people, but we are ultimately the ones responsible for our own happiness. This is because we can always decide how we see things and how we respond to them.

KEY TAKEAWAYS

- Self-disciplined people take responsibility for their lives, and instead of blaming others refrain from pointing fingers before understanding your situation.
- Whatever changes we seek, we must first take charge of our lives and never fully leave them to someone else. Accepting responsibility ultimately entails changing the direction of our lives in order to experience greater fulfillment and more beneficial outcomes.
- As explained above, there are some steps we can take to assume responsibilities, such as prioritizing ourselves, being wary of excuses, removing toxic people, focusing on taking action, loving ourselves, getting rid of negative self-talk, acknowledging the existence of negative emotions, and not internalizing judgment.
- In American culture, responsibility and fault often go hand in hand. However, they are two different things. The fault is in the past; responsibility is in the present. This is why when you take responsibility for something it does not mean that it is necessarily your fault. Taking responsibility means that we agree to be responsible to fix the problems so we can become better.

7

PRACTICING DELAYED GRATIFICATION

"The ability to discipline yourself to delay gratification in the short term in order to enjoy greater rewards in the long term, is the indispensable prerequisite for success."- Brian Tracy

WHAT IS DELAYED GRATIFICATION?

Having something that we desire right away feels great. However, there are times when doing something to feel good or to prevent discomfort costs us what we really want out of life. These longer-term objectives serve as a reward for delayed gratification. The goals do not even have to be that far into the future, yet they can bring us greater happiness or shield us from more suffering than the gratification we get from the present moment.

What exactly is delayed gratification? It is the capacity to resist the temptation of immediate pleasure in hopes of a greater or even more lasting reward in the future (Waters, 2021). When we know how to delay gratification, we can hold off until we finally get what we really want. Its opposite is instant satisfaction; instead of being patient and waiting for what we really desire, we choose something that will make us happy immediately.

Instant gratification is accepted as the norm in the age of one-click transactions and instantly available information. The idea that we must have what we want immediately is reinforced by the tech world where we have our internet and smartphones at all times. Instant gratification, however, is not always the greatest option; in fact, delayed gratification is a crucial life skill that we must learn. When it comes to having consistent self-discipline to reach our goals, delayed gratification is an ability that will get us there more quickly.

The truth is that expecting to achieve everything we desire, much less instantly, is impossible. Since it raises unrealistic expectations, instant gratification is essentially a starting point of frustration. Developing the ability to delay gratification allows us to gain time to plan things carefully and also learn from our failures.

The Marshmallow Test

THE MARSHMALLOW TEST

Walter Mischel, a professor at Stanford, came up with one of the better examples of delayed gratification in the 1960s (Robbins, 2022). He experimented on young children by putting every one of them in a room with just a marshmallow on a table. He then made a deal with every kid that if they held off on eating the marshmallow while he momentarily left the room, he would give them another marshmallow. However, there would not be another marshmallow if the child decided to eat the first one.

The findings of the infamous Marshmallow Test showed how challenging it is for humans of all ages to delay gratification. Some kids gobbled up the first marshmallow right away. Others made an effort to exercise self-control but ended up giving up. Only a handful of kids were able to resist and receive the second marshmallow prize.

The researchers then followed the Marshmallow Test participants into adulthood for over 40 years (Navidad, 2020). The kids who chose to delay their reward were much more successful in practically all aspects of their lives than those who gave in to the first marshmallow. Moreover, they also possessed greater social skills, became healthier, performed better on their tests, reacted much better to anxiety and stress, as well as had fewer drug problems (Robbins, 2022). This illustration of delayed gratification showed how important it is to reach our goals and accomplish more in essentially every area of life.

HERE ARE A FEW OF THE BENEFITS OF PRACTICING DELAYED GRATIFICATION

ACHIEVING LONG-TERM SUCCESS

When pursuing long-term objectives in both our personal and professional lives, we often have to make certain decisions. Do we spend our time watching a YouTube video or completing our homework? Should we waste our money on new clothes or save it for a nicer apartment? Do we choose to browse through Instagram or finish our project at work? Choosing what seems harder suggests at least some form of delayed gratification. More benefits result from doing so regularly than we would get in the short term. We will be able to achieve success over longer periods when we are willing to give up the pleasure we are currently enjoying in order to work toward our future goals. Delaying gratification allows us to hit more of our long-term targets and thus demonstrate to ourselves that we are capable of completing these tasks. We may feel better about ourselves as a result. For example, when you have a project assigned to you, you will want to create high-quality work within the time frame given to make your superior satisfied. In order to achieve that goal, you will need to avoid postponing doing the project and pour your heart into it. Once you are able to present great work and get complimented because of it, you will feel good about yourself and trust your ability more than before, which leads to greater self-worth.

HAVING IMPROVED HEALTH

In the Marshmallow Test, it was discovered that children who were more open to waiting for long periods for their reward would go on to have better long-term health. This is perhaps because they have the ability to delay gratification rather than fall into the temptation of bad behaviors. For instance, they may be more skilled at controlling their urges to smoke, consume unhealthy foods, put off exercising, and drink excessively.

GREATER MENTAL STABILITY

As you consolidate your ability to chase long-term rewards instead of short-term distractions, you'll also improve your mental health and well-being. Once you demonstrate a greater mental stability, staying the course to achieve distant goals becomes much easier.

Nevertheless, you will gain a new level of emotional intelligence.

EXAMPLES OF DELAYED GRATIFICATION

What does delayed gratification appear like? Depending on the area of life, it can take many different forms. Let's examine several instances of delayed gratification so that we can practice it more.

PERSONAL LIFE

Regardless of our weight, improving our nutrition is a long-term commitment that can help us become healthier as we age. However, it calls for a great deal of delayed gratification. It may feel nice at the moment to overeat or indulge in tempting foods that do not properly nourish our bodies. The greater reward, though, is healthy nourishment, which is difficult to attain for a lot of people. Put differently, we get to experience the gratification of being healthier as opposed to constantly consuming tasty but unhealthy meals and feeling satisfied for a moment only. We, therefore, have to be able to resist the need to indulge in unhealthy foods right away and focus on our long-term goals of maintaining good health.

PROFESSIONAL LIFE

Let's say that we are working to get a promotion at work. We are all aware that in order to accomplish this, we will have to hone the skills that define a strong leader. Even when we do not always feel like doing it, we must develop these skills outside of work if we want to see some improvement. It is very easy to fall prey to instant gratification and waste our evenings binge-watching our favorite TV programs. However, doing that will not pay off in the long term. Rather, we will need to invest some time in improving ourselves in order to receive the greater advantage of a promotion. This can help us develop as a leader and increase our likelihood of attaining our long-term professional ambitions.

INTERPERSONAL LIFE

There is an equal amount of giving and receiving in any healthy relationship. Our needs cannot always come first when we are trying to develop a relationship with somebody else. We may occasionally have to give in so as to build a long-lasting partnership that is advantageous to both sides. If someone they care about needs them, those with an instant gratification mentality may prioritize their own needs over their partner's. Delaying gratification, on the contrary, enables both sides to cooperate in order to create a positive, equal partnership.

THE STEPS TO BECOMING BETTER AT DELAYING GRATIFICATION

Delaying gratification is difficult at a time when distractions are all around us. It can be challenging to resist the temptation of Facebook, Instagram, TikTok, and Netflix. When companies are competing for our valuable attention, how can we maintain our discipline? In order to answer this question, here are some steps that can be utilized in order to be better at delaying gratification.

KNOWING WHAT YOU WANT

Everybody aspires to success, but not everyone actually accomplishes it. We need to first determine our intentions and desires in order to increase our chances. Finding a goal from our current passions is a fantastic place to start, and here are a few examples:

- Having money and material possessions.
- Obtaining a happy state of mind.
- Preserving physical health.
- Positively impacting others.
- Exploring or learning something new.
- Being efficient with time and productive.
- Establishing connections and making acquaintances.

What do you think your life's work is? Commit to your goals by putting them in writing. The actual work starts once we have made up our minds about what we want to achieve in life.

BEGINNING WITH A SMALL THING

It is not necessary to begin exercising our ability to delay gratification because of something that will happen years from now. We should start off small and work toward our larger, longer-term objectives after that. The gratification for a small thing should still be delayed, even though we only have to wait a short period of time before receiving it. How long we should wait relies on our capacity for delayed gratification. For example, if we struggle to wait a week for a reward, we may start with one day only. As time passes by, we will be able to incorporate the habit into our lives gradually. If we do not have anything specific we want to work toward, we can establish it in our lives.

Here is one instance. Say you want to get better at public speaking at your office. Your practice will not immediately provide good results. However, you may give yourself a break by doing something enjoyable as a reward for practicing public speaking every day. This can involve watching an episode of your favorite Netflix show. As a consequence, if you do not practice, it means that you cannot watch any episode that day; then you will have to wait another day to get that reward. You can then increase your tolerance as time goes on. Perhaps following a couple of weeks of honing your public speaking skill, you can reward yourself with a trip to the spa or the salon.

TAKING A BREAK FROM SOCIAL MEDIA

This may appear to have nothing to do with delayed gratification, but it is actually not true. When was the last time you went through Instagram or Facebook without ending up at an external website to look at an online shop? Social media influencers have a reason for doing what they do on the internet, and these apps were purposefully created with that in mind. Since social media is a relatable thing for people of all ages, it is the most effective kind of marketing. The more we browse through it, the more we will feel as though we need a product to be as happy as the people we see on the internet. For instance, a lot of us are probably guilty of buying unnecessary skincare and beauty products in an effort to resemble our favorite social media influencers.

However, if we desire to learn to delay gratification, removing a key stimulus for routinely gratifying ourselves instantly is a terrific way to do this. For instance, we can perhaps take a week or two off social media. As another example, if Instagram is a major trigger for us, we can take it further by deactivating or deleting our account. We need to be aware of how it impacts our impulses. Once we are aware of these triggers and impulses, we can avoid them much better and learn to put off our urges for delayed gratification.

THINKING ABOUT THE REAL COST

Asking ourselves this question will allow us to delay gratification more successfully: What does the thing or the action we are going to perform actually cost? For instance, if we are about to make a significant purchase from an online shop, we can make an effort to estimate how many hours of work it will need. We will start to second-guess ourselves when we realize that one item might equal a week of work to do. As another illustration, if we are about to consume a whole bucket of ice cream in one sitting, we have to think of all the possible costs to our health. This can result in a significant blood sugar increase that will undoubtedly result in various stomach problems. The real cost of instant reward may not always be worth it at all. We all need to think about the cost and decide if the momentary pleasure is actually worth it to us.

KEY TAKEAWAYS

- Delayed gratification refers to the ability to resist the temptation of immediate pleasure. We avoid temptation because we anticipate a bigger or longer-lasting reward down the road.

- As demonstrated by the Marshmallow Test, the children who decided to wait for more rewards became more successful in their lives as they grew up. This is because they knew how to control their impulses and did not give in to instant gratification easily. From this experiment, we learn how important it is to practice delayed gratification more in our lives.

- There are some benefits that can be gained from practicing delayed gratification, such as achieving stronger self-worth, having improved health, and getting long-term success.

- Tips on becoming better at delaying gratification: knowing what you want, beginning with a small thing, taking a break from social media, and thinking about the real cost. If we follow these tips, we will be able to wait for better future rewards, which can lead to having consistent self-discipline as well.

8

IGNORING THE NAYSAYERS

"Ignore the naysayers. They don't know what they're talking about when it comes to your life."- Maria Lesetz

WHAT ARE NAYSAYERS?

Naysayers are people who like to express their negative or pessimistic views and project them onto others (Khurana, 2021). No matter where we are on the grand game board of life, we will encounter individuals who, to put it bluntly, have less-than-good motives at some point. We will always have those people rooting for us, like our family and friends, who support whatever we do. They want to be present to share our achievements with us because they want those things for us and are confident they will happen in the first place. But there are also some who are being negative about everything. They constantly seem to be in our lives and enjoy pointing out our shortcomings and how we will fail in what we dream to accomplish.

When we tell the naysayers what we wish for in life, they often start doubting us and our ability to succeed, thus discouraging us from even attempting to try something. They typically lack the knowledge necessary to determine our chances of success, but they will try to talk us out of our plans and convince us that we will fail. It truly does not matter what these negative people think and what their opinions are, regardless of their motivations. Oftentimes, they will advise against trying something since they tried it and ended in failure. But someone is not automatically an expert just because they tried it once, failed to achieve it, and decided to give up.

Even while there is a general sense that things are going well, a few naysayers will try to cast pessimism, which can result in hindering our progress. Every time we are getting sidetracked by naysayers, it is simply because we have lost focus on the goals that we have set. If so, all we have to do is take a look at them again. We need to remind ourselves what we desire to do specifically. We must also think about what it is that we truly wish for our lives. If we are dealing with naysayers, we have to first realize that we are in control of our own lives and do not need negative people telling us what we must do.

Arnold Schwarzenegger has taken to heart Nelson Mandela's belief that "It always seems to be impossible until someone does it." Schwarzenegger wanted to break new records and do something that no one else had ever done, and he actually accomplished what he set out to do. What he did seemed impossible, and he probably had to ignore a couple of naysayers, but he kept going until he achieved what he wanted.

THE REASONS TO IGNORE THE NAYSAYERS

STOPPING NEGATIVITY FROM CREEPING INTO YOUR MIND

The strength of positive thinking is real. Although it might sound like a thing from fictional stories, a lot can actually be achieved simply by maintaining a positive mindset. This way of thinking keeps us going when things get tough and also makes us stay away from the naysayers in the process. By being optimistic, we will be able to persuade people to support us or change their minds, which will let us take control of the matter. For the precise reason that it fosters more success, some people even describe a positive attitude as a development mindset (Olenski, 2018).

For example, great leaders have a method of preventing negativity from affecting them. In the business world, all sorts of unpleasant events might occur, but leaders cannot allow these things to get them down. If a leader always appears depressed, angry, displeased, or sad, their team will not be able to count on them to be the presence that the team members need. To great leaders, naysayers cannot be fully ignored because occasionally they may provide insightful feedback. However, rather than dwelling on that negativity, great leaders will first recognize the perspective before turning to a more positive path. Negativity can consume our entire being if we let it because it serves only as a roadblock on the way to our success.

PREVENTING YOU FROM ABANDONING YOUR DREAM

Nobody wants to wonder about what could have occurred if they had pursued their goal rather than just letting somebody convince them not to do it. This kind of regret will lead us to hatred and resentment. If we realize that somebody else uses that idea that we have thought about, proceeded with it, and is now incredibly successful, we can feel upset and resentful.

We all know about Jeff Bezos, the founder of Amazon and one of the richest men on earth. He once said that he knew that if he had failed, he would not have regretted that, but a thing he would definitely regret was not trying at all. Even though we may dislike and even hate the person who persuaded us that our goals will never come true, we will resent ourselves even more for following their opinion and allowing them to determine our lives' fate. If Jeff Bezos and his vision of the greatest online shop in the world have turned out to be successful, there is no excuse we cannot accomplish our own ambitions by not listening to the naysayers.

MOTIVATING OTHER PEOPLE TO IGNORE THEIR NAYSAYERS

We can serve as a motivation and role model for others with our relentless determination to achieve success in the face of difficulties. For example, internet influencers these days have become a crucial part of modern marketing because what reputable people do and say is shaping more and more how individuals make decisions in their lives. While influencers frequently affect people's shopping choices, they can also be a factor in different kinds of decisions, such as whether or not someone should transform an idea into a real business.

For instance, if we aspire to instill motivation in business for others, a great way to start is to volunteer as a mentor to young entrepreneurs. We can try to share our success stories in various schools and online learning classes. We may also join a mentorship group to help others who are dealing with the same naysayers get beyond the obstacles just as we did. Moreover, if we want to become social media influencers, we can open up an Instagram or YouTube account and post videos about our success journeys there. We will be able to influence other people positively by paving our own path to success first.

WAYS TO IGNORE THE NAYSAYERS

DEFINING YOUR DREAM CLEARLY

We will be more likely to stick to our goals in the face of challenges if we describe them clearly. We need to be more specific here. What precisely does the dream look like? How will we know when we have succeeded in reaching our goals? We have to clearly envisage this. For example, if you are good at programming and wish to create a new game, you will have to know what kind of game you want to make. You need to think about how the game will play out and where the market you want to promote it is. Perhaps you will think that you have reached the goal when the game is finished being programmed or when it brings you some profits. When you can define your goal, it will be much easier for you to start.

KNOWING WHY YOU ARE DOING IT

Why is this dream important? There is no correct response to this question. Simply being able to respond to it and having an answer that inspires us to take action is what matters. Our motivation to keep going will increase when our reasons for wanting to realize our ambitions become stronger. Let's take the example above. You wish to create a new game, but why do you want to do this? What is your endgame? Do you wish to get as much profit as possible and make your own game company? Do you only do it for fun because it is your passion? Whatever your reasons, you need to know them first.

FIGHTING YOUR INNER NAYSAYERS

We might be the worst critic of ourselves. Our inner naysayers are the voice inside of us telling us we will not be able to accomplish our future goals because we are not clever enough, wealthy enough, lucky enough, or connected with the right people, among other things. We must silence all these negative voices and replace them with one that is empowering in reminding us that we can do everything because we are smart, hard-working, and strong enough to accomplish it.

SURROUNDING YOURSELF WITH POSITIVE INDIVIDUALS

In large part, we will become just like the people we are with. We will probably become negative people if we only hang out with negative individuals in our lives. We will benefit from surrounding ourselves with people who are pursuing their goals, facing their fears, and improving their skills. The people we choose to have around us play a big role in determining who we are or want to be. When you were young, your parents may have warned you not to hang out with the kids who drank alcohol or did drugs because they might have a bad influence on you. Your parents were definitely in the right here since these kids would try to convince others to do what they did or you would think that you were not cool enough if you did not engage in these activities.

NOT THINKING ABOUT YOUR PLANS TOO MUCH

Planning too much is not good because actions are actually much more crucial than plans. We should not get too caught up in having the ideal plan before we start because 99.9% of every plan ends up changing as we are doing it. We need to make a move as soon as we can. We should start when the idea pops up in our heads and make changes later on. As long as we are clear in defining our goals, we will be able to accomplish them successfully. For instance, you want to make a clothing business and have made all the designs. You may also know what materials you would like to use on the clothes. In this scenario, you should just start finding tailors to make samples for your clothes instead of thinking about it too much. On the way, if you do not like how the designs are or you think that the materials are not good enough, you can just change them as you see fit before finally ordering the final products.

BEING READY TO FAIL

Failure is not a thing because it does not exist; instead, there are just outcomes. It is as simple as that to take new action if the previous ones do not produce the desired results. We need to get over our failure-related fears. We should get out there and fail quickly and frequently so that we can learn from our mistakes and advance as time passes. We should never stop trying because we do not get what we want on the first try. What we should do is try again, no matter how many times we make mistakes. Let's take a look at Suzy Batiz, for example. Batiz experienced two periods of bankruptcy prior to founding the $240 million brand Poo-Pourri toilet spray (Castrillon, 2019). She sought to start a business from scratch, as she was enthusiastic about the industry. However, that did not work out at first because, at the age of 21, she made her first bankruptcy filing. Batiz refused to give in to the difficult circumstances. She established the Poo-Pourri toilet spray business after filing for bankruptcy for the second time, and it became a big success. She ultimately managed to rank among America's Richest Self-Made Women in 2019 as a result of her company's good advertising strategy (Castrillon, 2019).

KEY TAKEAWAYS

- If we wish to accomplish our goals and have consistent self-discipline, we will have to ignore all the naysayers that are around us. All they do is bring negativity into our lives and hinder our future success.
- Naysayers want us to believe that our ideas and ambitions are just in our heads and are not possible to put into action. This is why we need to remove them from our lives so that we will become more positive and will not have any regrets later on.
- Tips for ignoring the naysayers: defining your dream clearly, knowing why you are pursuing it, fighting your inner naysayers, surrounding yourself with positive individuals, not thinking about your plans too much, and being ready to fail.

9

FINDING A MENTOR TO EMULATE

"A mentor empowers a person to see a possible future, and believe it can be obtained."- Shawn Hitchcock

In a mentoring relationship, an experienced person (the mentor) shares their knowledge, skills, and wisdom with a less experienced person (the mentee) all while developing their own mentoring abilities (D'Angelo, 2022). In mentorship, proper guidance is provided to the mentee while still keeping a friendly and encouraging relationship with the mentor.

Someone can be considered a mentor when they have succeeded in the goal that we wish to achieve. It means that they have mastered the ways to have consistent self-discipline in order to accomplish that goal. Therefore, if we set a goal, it is essential that we find ourselves a mentor who can give us advice and tips on how to accomplish it. When we have little experience, we may occasionally feel confused when pursuing our goals. A mentor, however, has years or decades of practical experience in our field and can help us develop our abilities and learn valuable lessons from (Roepe, 2022). Finding a mentor then is one of the most powerful moves we can do to change our lives.

THE BENEFITS OF HAVING A MENTOR

There are several advantages to mentoring for us. We can discover new things, expand our networks, and improve our self-discipline by establishing this relationship. We can determine whether or not we wish to find a mentor by considering these benefits.

HAVING SOMEONE TO SUPPORT YOUR GROWTH

Mentors support and empower the growth of another person's improvement. A mentor can help us to concentrate our efforts by providing feedback and setting goals. For this reason, many companies often develop mentorship programs in order to hone the skills of their employees. Employees like working environments that support professional growth because it shows that their employer cares about them and intends to see them succeed.

TAPPING INTO A SOURCE OF KNOWLEDGE

Mentors can offer us specialized knowledge and perspectives that help us succeed. They provide guidance on how to carry out specific tasks or acquire practical skills, for instance. Such advice can be helpful to those who are just starting their professional careers because it enables them to become more at ease in their positions more quickly and perhaps get promoted more easily. For example, you are about to start a new company. When you have a mentor on your side, they will be able to teach you how to create your preliminary business and financial plan. It means that you will not have to spend so much time researching about it because your mentor can provide it for you easily.

MAINTAINING ACCOUNTABILITY

Mentors support their mentees by holding them accountable for their goals. A mentor can keep us motivated and on course to fulfill our goals by monitoring our progress as we go along. In addition, they can make sure that we do not lose sight of our ambitions. Having someone who keeps an eye on us can help to motivate and hold us accountable since we do not want to disappoint our mentors by failing to accomplish our goals. For example, if you start to procrastinate or get discouraged in your efforts, a mentor will remind you why you need to keep going because you need to be responsible for yourself and your life.

PROVIDING ENCOURAGEMENT

We can seek assistance from our mentors when we are having trouble completing a task or achieving a goal. We may be inspired to keep going forward in the face of obstacles by this support and encouragement. In order to instill confidence in us, our mentors might also recognize and remind us of our strengths and skills. When we can radiate confidence, we will be less inclined to give up on our ambitions and dreams.

HELPING CREATE NEW CONNECTIONS

A mentor can support us in expanding our network and connection. They can introduce us to potential opportunities or people who will be able to help us when we can identify our career or personal goals. For example, if we want career advancement at work, these kinds of connections are helpful for us because our mentors often have more experience in the business or more senior positions as well. A mentor can lead us to the right people in pursuit of our goals so that we do not have to start from the beginning by ourselves.

HAVING SOMEONE WILLING TO LISTEN TO YOU

When we get an idea in our heads, we can share it with a mentor to discuss or debate it. Thanks to their relevant knowledge and experience, a mentor can provide us with honest guidance and suggestions about what we need to do. These insights help us decide whether or not to go along with that idea or abandon it, as well as what strategies to take. Furthermore, a mentor can also assist us with day-to-day issues. For example, if you have a project-related conflict with your boss at work, you can turn to your mentor for guidance on what measures to take because they will listen to you before offering advice.

GETTING CONSTRUCTIVE FEEDBACK

Genuine feedback can be given in a mentoring relationship built on trust. By developing trust, we will be able to learn that constructive feedback from our mentors is meant to advance our development instead of hurting our personal feelings. Our mentors can help us by pointing out areas for improvement and any shortcomings we might need to overcome. Since this is a professional connection, our mentors have objective roles to fulfill. Our friends or colleagues can be reluctant to point up our flaws because they do not want to come off as judgmental. For example, if you have an impossible idea that you think will work out, your friends may not be willing to talk too much about it lest you take their words the wrong way and think that they are being negative to you. However, a mentor will be able to give you honest comments on the idea since you trust them and their intentions.

PROVIDING GUIDELINES

If we have just started our careers, a mentor can help us establish guidelines for what is expected of us professionally. For instance, they might make clear the importance of the position and acceptable workplace conduct. These guidelines may assist us in forming productive work habits that will help us concentrate and complete our tasks successfully. We will be able to increase our productivity and impress our bosses with these productive work practices.

HAVING A TRUSTED ALLY

A crucial aspect of mentoring partnerships is trust. We have to have faith in our mentors and trust that they will offer accurate and sincere advice as well as have our best interests in mind. We both must be able to rely on each other to keep secret information private. In order to build trust in the relationship, our mentors have to be able to keep their word and communicate frequently. For instance, if you are planning to implement a new business idea and run it by your mentor, they will have to keep all information about it confidential so that no one can steal that idea from you. Given how fierce the competition is in the business sector, a mentor whom we can trust is very important to have.

HOW TO FIND AND ESTABLISH A RELATIONSHIP WITH A MENTOR

KNOWING WHAT A MENTOR IS AND IS NOT

As explained above, a mentor is an individual who can support and empower us, urge us to seek out new prospects, and assist us in overcoming obstacles, such as changing roles or accepting a difficult job. For example, a mentor may be someone who works in the same field as us or a person in the profession type of role we wish to change into. This person can serve as our mentor and provide advice on how to enhance our careers or work. Although it is possible to receive mentorship from a friend, generally mentors will be at least one or two career levels higher than us (Patel, 2022). We need to remember that a mentor is not the same as a sponsor. A sponsor utilizes their connections to actively support a younger or less experienced individual's professional progress, while a mentor provides guidance and addresses concerns (Roepe, 2022).

We generally think of mentorship as a long-term, one-on-one connection between a mentor and mentee, but that is actually not the only possibility. Peer mentoring with somebody on the same level as us and group mentoring where we do not meet one-on-one are only two examples of the various types of mentoring available out there (Krbechek & Tagle, 2022). Additionally, mentoring can be done on small levels. For example, you look up to a colleague at work who has a good performance. In order to learn more about their experiences or to get advice on how to perform better at work, you can ask them to have a one-time mentoring session with you.

BEING SPECIFIC ABOUT YOUR GOAL

We should think about what we intend to gain from the partnership before we even begin to consider asking a person to be our mentor. The purpose of our mentoring relationships might be to aid us in overcoming a transition or obstacle or to improve in an area where we require additional assistance or direction, but it's up to us to figure it out.

For example, in your workplace, if your manager has urged you to work on being more persuasive in meetings with clients, you should consider which of your coworkers can help you master that skill. Perhaps you have been entrusted with drafting your first marketing strategy so you are looking for pointers from someone else, or you want to apply for a new position or promotion and need some advice on how to move forward in your professional life.

DISCOVERING THE RIGHT MENTOR

Once we have identified the skills and goals we need assistance with, or what questions we have about our work, we should look around our community—including our families, friends, or colleagues—for potential mentors. In the workplace, our mentors do not have to be someone in an executive position, nor do they have to be much older than we. Somebody who is only four to five years our senior might have better insight and provide more useful guidance o since they tend to be more familiar with the daily challenges faced by an individual in our position (Roepe, 2022).

For instance, if you are a programmer seeking to advance into management, you can try to get in touch with your college roommate, with whom you always got along well, and who has been serving as a programming manager for a while. As another example, if you are an entry-level salesperson seeking to specialize in social media, you can consider reaching out to the social media coordinator you have met during a previous internship.

REACHING OUT AND BUILDING A RELATIONSHIP

It is usually preferable to ask a mutual contact to introduce us to a potential mentor if we want to ask somebody we do not know to be our mentor. If we do not have a mutual friend to connect us to that person, it is crucial to first build a common ground before we reach out to them. For instance, we can mention that we attended the same college as them, work in the same field, or are members of the same professional association.

If we have never met a potential mentor, we should tell them what we admire about their work. We have to familiarize ourselves with the work of that person and all the things they have done in their field. Then, we can start praising something about their work. This way, we can show that we have a thoughtful approach when trying to get to know them and ask for their help. We can then begin telling them about ourselves, our work and goals, and the reasons we are contacting them. For example, we can say, "I recently received a promotion to marketing manager, and I want to enhance my readiness for my new position. Would you mind if I ask a few questions regarding how to further develop my skills for the new role?"

MAKING THINGS EASY FOR YOUR MENTOR

We also need to be considerate of our mentors' time by handling the logistics, such as arranging a meeting location or a Skype call, so they can simply show up and provide their guidance. In order to give our mentors time to plan how to best assist us, we should also email them an outline or our list of questions the day prior to our appointment. If our mentors set a one-hour limit for the meeting, we must always be on time and considerate of the time they can spare for us. If we are meeting them in person, we also have to pay for their coffee or food.

LETTING THEM KNOW THAT YOU VALUE THEIR FEEDBACK

If our mentor advises us to take a certain course of action or read a particular book, we should be able to show them that we are implementing their advice by sharing the results of doing so with them via email or at our following meeting. Moreover, we need to follow up on the latter by sharing the lessons we have learned from them. For example, if we read an article that we think our mentor will find useful, we should forward it to them and explain how it connects to a previous discussion that we had.

KEY TAKEAWAYS

- It sounds cliché, but you are the sum of the 5 people you hang around the most. Whether you like it or not, you will be significantly influenced by people who are close to you.
- If you want to change your (work) life for the better, a mentor can be a valuable asset. Having a mentor can benefit you in many ways, from having someone to support your growth, listen to you, and give you constructive feedback to tapping into a source of knowledge, gaining encouragement, helping create new connections, and having a trusted ally.
- Some tips on looking for a mentor and building a relationship with them: knowing what a mentor is, being specific about your goal, discovering the right mentor, reaching out to your mentor, and letting them know that you value their time and feedback.

10

MOTIVATION IS A FEELING THAT COMES AND GOES

"Motivation is fickle. It comes and goes. It is unreliable and when you are counting on motivation to get your goals accomplished – you will likely fall short." – Jocko Willink

MOTIVATION IS NOT A RELIABLE EMOTION

Motivation is one of the buzzwords that is used rather frequently nowadays, specifically when it comes to media advertising. We all have seen various commercials about it, not to mention the countless social media articles and posts that come up on our feeds. Most of the time, in real life, people will say things like, "I am not feeling motivated," or "how do I become more motivated?"

There are days when none of us want to do anything. Perhaps we had a challenging workday, or perhaps we are just feeling lazy and would rather stay in bed all day long. Whatever the cause, it is quite simple to lose motivation these days. From here, we realize that motivation is just an emotion.

Successful people do not believe in motivation as a concept. I personally believe in self-discipline because it always helped me along the way. People who are counting on motivation basically are saying: "I don't feel like doing this. How do I feel like doing this?" And the answer is that you are never going to feel like doing this all the time. This is deeply embedded in human nature.

I remember when I was going to the gym there were days when I simply wasn't motivated to get out of bed even if I enjoyed working out a lot.

If I were to tell you to go skydiving or driving a luxury car every day, there are going to be mornings when you wake up and you just don't feel like doing it, no matter how fun it is. That's life. If you count on motivation, you will never perform against people who act despite how they feel. You must make a decision. Forget about the idea of motivation, throw it away and decide who you are. For me, I decided to be a winner, and I know what it takes to win. To win, I must perform day after day regardless of how I feel. Some days I will enjoy it, some days I will not. However, I don't allow my emotional state to affect my actions. Let's say you are a soccer player and you have a game on March 1st. That day comes and you might feel like you are going to scale and give your best in the game, or you might feel the opposite. But all the tickets are sold, the contracts are signed and nobody cares if you don't feel like doing it. You must be good enough on your worst day to beat your opponent on his best days.

After reading this paragraph take 10 minutes and go look in the mirror and decide who you are going to be. Are you a loser? Because if you are, you can read and watch a variety of motivational speeches, trying to convince yourself to do a bit of work. But in the long run it will be pointless. Or are you a winner?

Motivation is a feeling similar to joy, sadness, anger, or frustration. As with any other emotion, it also can come and go suddenly and for no apparent reason. It is the same as how we can experience moments of happiness, followed by anger. Motivation can change and fade away, as when we may be so utterly irritated at someone initially only to find them funny just moments later; or when we prepare our clothes the night before because we are so excited to hit the gym early in the morning, only to realize that when the alarm goes off at 6 a.m., that is the last place we would like to be, and we just want to stay in bed longer; or when we have prepared for a singing audition months beforehand, but when the day comes to perform, we cannot seem to bring ourselves to attend it anymore. In all of these instances, we simply lose our motivation.

Since we have recognized that motivation is just an emotion, it is not reliable at all. We should not use it as the basis of our decisions and actions in our lives. For example, if you build your marriage with your partner solely around the feeling of passionate attraction, you will be in a lot of trouble when the stress and financial worries set in, and you also have to deal with your children's conflicting schedules. As another example, if you have kids and you base your parenting on never getting annoyed by them, things will not turn out well because raising them can be frustrating and stressful most of the time. You cannot be a good partner or parent if you only rely on motivation when establishing your relationship or raising children.

DISCIPLINE IS FAR MORE IMPORTANT THAN

MOTIVATION

In the end, what distinguishes successful individuals from unsuccessful ones is that they are being disciplined enough to do things even when they are not motivated. It is more crucial to be self-disciplined than to feel motivated, particularly when it comes to long-term objectives. Once we have developed the habit of discipline, we can use it even when we do not feel motivated at all. This is essential because, over time, discipline will enable us to stick to and eventually accomplish our goals even when we do not have any motivation to take action.

Anybody who has ever attempted to accomplish a difficult goal is aware of how important discipline is. When it comes to achieving our goals, discipline is necessary regardless of whether we want to exercise, eat well, or study for a test. The explanation for this is very straightforward: Momentum stems from discipline. The easier anything gets, the more disciplined we are; as a result, we will also build up more momentum (Rothwell, 2022). What was once challenging eventually turns into a habit, and habits are tough to break. Because discipline is essential to bringing about long-lasting change, it is necessary to practice it consistently. Discipline is what enables us to withstand unpleasant feelings, stay on course, and make adjustments in line with our established plans rather than as a result of emotional reactions (Robinson, 2022).

We need to rely on self-discipline because plans are harder to implement than to establish. As an illustration, if you plan to have a healthier lifestyle, you will have to create habits and stick to them– from prepping nutritious homemade meals throughout the week, saying no sugary drinks or alcohol, and eating sufficient protein to working out at the gym 3 times a week, going for a walk, and sleeping enough during the night. You have to do these activities day in and day out in order to make them into habits.

You should not rely on motivation alone because it can disappear in the course of the long journey; rather, you will need to show self-discipline if you want to reach the goal of having a healthier lifestyle. In conclusion, although motivation is an excellent starting point, it is necessary to keep in mind that it will not stay forever. Utilizing motivation to make it through the day can be an up-and-down roller coaster for us.

Moreover, even though maintaining discipline through daily routines and habits may appear boring, we are actually making progress every day. When we practice self-discipline in one area of our lives, it naturally extends and moves to other aspects of our lives, which will surprise us.

HOW TO KEEP GOING EVEN WHEN YOU ARE NOT MOTIVATED

Everybody experiences days when they lack the motivation to function or even get out of bed. It is common to experience these feelings occasionally. It is possible that we are under stress because of a task at our workplace or a personal problem. Whatever the cause, it is important to keep in mind that these emotions are temporary because they will eventually pass. When we are lacking motivation, we can try these things to get through the day:

- Taking a break: When we feel down or unmotivated, we need to leave what we are doing where we are at. We can try going for a stroll, turning on some music, opening a book, or cooking our favorite meal. Whatever activity we choose, we need to ensure that they can calm us down. We must set aside some time for rest and rejuvenation. Once our minds are relaxed, we will be able to focus on what things are necessary to finish.

- Transcending our environment: Occasionally, a change of setting is all that is required. If we work from home, we can consider visiting a coffee shop or a public park. Changing our surroundings can help our creativity take off if we are stuck. If we work from the office, we can declutter our workspace or even decorate it with all the things we like. When we feel happy with our environment, it will be much easier to work through our tasks.
- Talking to someone: When we are feeling low, talking to someone can be therapeutic and beneficial. This can facilitate the processing of our emotions and the creation of an action plan that we need. By speaking with a friend or a member of our family, we will also feel supported and cared for. Our loved ones may provide us with solutions or advice for our issues, as well as with emotional support.
- Taking action: Oftentimes taking action is the greatest way to break out of a block. We can try to start that task we have been putting off, or take a stroll around our neighborhood. Doing something, no matter how small or trivial, may be able to help us get out of our mind block.
- Using Inspiration: Inspiration is stronger than motivation. We are inspired to take action when we encounter something which inspires us. For example, when we witness someone else achieve their dream of establishing their own company, we are inspired to do the same. This is why it is essential to surround ourselves with people who can inspire us and look for new inspiration as well.

Once we become more self-disciplined, we will begin to see the outcomes we seek. However, we must be cautious to limit the number of these strenuous days to avoid feeling burnt out. By following the steps outlined above, we can keep working toward our goals productively.

KEY TAKEAWAYS

- Discipline accounts for 99% of the job we are doing, and motivation for the remaining 1%. This is why this chapter is teaching us not to rely solely on motivation.
- As motivation comes and goes, we should focus our energy on developing our self-discipline instead.
- Successful people already realize how important it is to keep going even when they do not feel motivated, and that is because they have self-discipline.
- Our emotions are temporary. When you are feeling low, keep in mind these four hacks: taking a break, transcending your environment, talking to someone, taking action, and using inspiration.

11

BUILDING HEALTHY HABITS

"Extraordinary habits are what allow people to perform at an elite level."- Ed Mylett

STARTING SMALL WITH ATOMIC HABITS

Do you want to improve the quality of your life and become more self-disciplined? That is fantastic, but you cannot accomplish this overnight. There is a process to follow, and we all must be prepared to put in the necessary effort. It is possible to build productive and healthy habits, and we need to start small for that.

James Clear, an expert on long-term habit development, asserts in his book *Atomic Habits* that by making minor alterations to our daily routines, we may be able to create good habits and also break negative ones (Goeke, 2018). In another sense, if we learn a small habit, or atomic habit, and practice it consistently, we can make incredible improvements in our lives. Atomic habits are small, recurring behaviors that are easy to pick up and maintain yet have a significant impact on how we conduct our daily lives (Clear, 2018).

TAKING IT STEP BY STEP

We should choose a new habit that is so small and simple that it does not need much effort to get done. One percent gains mount up quite quickly as well as one percent drops. Instead of attempting something extraordinary right away, we should start small and get better over time (Clear, 2022). For example, if we want to start doing sit-ups, we can try 5 on the first day, 6 on the second, 7 on the third, and so on. Likewise, if you want to build up your meditation to 30 minutes, start by dividing it into two stages of 15 minutes each. We have to make a habit simple enough so that we can do it easily without putting much effort in the beginning. Every habit needs to be manageable in order to keep momentum and make the action as simple as possible to carry out

(Clear, 2022). Our motivation and willpower will grow along the journey. As a result, it will be easier for us to maintain our habits in the long run.

GETTING BACK ON TRACK

Like everybody else in this world, top performers can make mistakes and stray from their intended path. The difference is that they get back on track as soon as they can. Although we should not expect to fail, we still have to prepare for those things that can get us off track. What are some common emergencies that can arise? How are we going to move past these problems? Or, at the very least, how can we efficiently recover from them and steady the course? Remember, we just have to be consistent, not perfect.

BUILDING HEALTHY HABITS IN 4 EASY STEPS

The fundamental steps that make up the habit-forming process are cue, craving, response, and reward. We can better comprehend what a habit is, how it functions, and how to change it by splitting it into these fundamental elements. Clear believes that the environment acts as an invisible force to mold human behavior when it comes to habits (Goeke, 2018). Therefore, the first action in establishing any habit is to always use a cue. Though it might not always be external, the majority of the time it will be. Each specific step of the four-stage pattern is described below.

- Cue: a clue that points to a potential reward, such as the aroma of baking cookies or a completely dark room that will shortly be lit up.
- Craving: the motivation to make a transformation so that we can reap the benefits, like tasting the cookie's deliciousness after baking them or being able to see when we turn on the light.
- Response: taking whatever steps or actions are necessary to reach the reward.

111

- Reward: the positive feeling we have as a result of the changes and the knowledge of whether to repeat it or not.

USING THE FOUR LAWS OF BEHAVIOR CHANGE

These four steps can be combined to create a useful framework that can create healthy habits and get rid of undesirable ones. Clear refers to this framework as the "four laws of behavior change" (Clear, 2018). Here they are, along with some suggestions for how to utilize them to foster positive behavior.

- Making it obvious: If we want to lead a healthier life, we should put the fruits we buy from the grocery store on display rather than hiding them at the back of our fridge.
- Making it attractive: When we are shopping for fruits, we should choose the ones that we truly enjoy eating so that when we see them, we will actually want to eat some.
- Making it easy: We should not create any unnecessary steps by choosing fruits that are more difficult to peel. For example, instead of choosing a watermelon, we can get a banana or an apple since they are very easy to eat.
- Making it satisfying: If we like the fruits we have bought, we will enjoy eating them and feel much healthier as a result.

These behaviors can support a variety of healthy habits, such as exercising, working on a side business, investing extra time with family, and so on. For a bad habit, on the other hand, we need to do the reverse. We should make it invisible, unattractive, difficult, and unsatisfying (Clear, 2018). We may, for instance, hide our cigarettes, impose fines, eliminate all lighters, and restrict our smoking time only outside, during cold nights.

HEALTHY HABITS YOU CAN BUILD NO MATTER WHAT YOUR GOALS ARE

NOT CHECKING YOUR PHONE FIRST THING IN THE MORNING

After waking up in the morning, we must try to keep our phone away and not check it for the first 30 minutes. We should instead use that time to accomplish something we deem more important. Some of these activities can be meditating for 15 minutes, taking a cold shower, writing down our goals, visualizing our future goals, and so forth. In addition, if not checking your phone in the morning turns out to be too much of a challenge, you can leave it in your car the night before.

KEEPING THE PROMISES YOU MAKE TO YOURSELF

Everyone who has experienced having a promise broken knows how frustrating or disappointing it can be. While keeping our promises to other people is a crucial component of a relationship, honoring our promise to ourselves is just as vital, if not more so. Every time we keep our word to ourselves, we demonstrate that we are reliable, that we honor our promise, and that we can depend on ourselves to meet our responsibilities. As a result, it will increase our self-confidence and self-esteem.

FOCUSING ON THE GOAL, NOT THE COST

We need to stop focusing on the cost and effort required to obtain our desired results and goals. For instance, we may need to purchase a course to help us expand our business or pick up a new talent, but we are unsure what to do when we see the price tag. We need to put an end to the negotiation; if the course can alter our lives for the better, it is definitely worthwhile. If we keep our eyes on the price tag only, we will inevitably give up on reaching our goals. Even if those around us tell us it will cost too much, we must fully commit to what we wish to accomplish.

GETTING LASER FOCUS

Procrastination is easily overcome if we can cultivate sufficient concentration skills. The ability to dedicate all of our mental energy to an activity we are actively prioritizing is known as laser focus. This allows us to shut out distractions, put all of our tempting, extraneous thoughts aside, and maintain the drive required to achieve our goals. One focusing strategy involves not just visualizing our dreams but also actively observing and learning from people who have reached theirs. Let's say you want to be a fitness model or influencer. You might attend sessions on bodybuilding, or follow influencers on social media to see what content they create and how. Or, if you're struggling to save the money you need to afford your dream car, you can go to a car dealership to test drive that car once in a while to see what it feels like to drive it.

OVERCOMING YOUR FEARS AND TAKING RISKS

We should never let fear dictate who we are or the things we are going to do. It is possible that we develop fears that are unnecessary, such as anxiety about public speaking. We can be hindered from moving forward in our work or taking part in activities, like making a toast at our closest friend's wedding due to our fear of public speaking. We need to take one little step at a time while facing our fears. When we are not ready, moving too quickly or doing something dangerous can backfire. We have to feel the fear first and keep moving forward slowly. It is okay to feel a little anxious.

By the same token, our opportunities are increased when we take risks and try new things. We will never get the chance to reach our goals if we insist on total safety and assurance. It is an uncomfortable truth, but in order to do anything worthwhile, we must act and venture into unfamiliar territory. Planning is the first step toward taking a risk. It involves searching within and asking yourself, "what do I really want?" Once we can answer this question, we should then make a strategy to get there and truly commit to turning it into a reality. When it involves achievement and goal-setting, taking reasonable, measured risks may be a game-changer.

WRITING DOWN ALL THE GOOD THINGS IN YOUR LIFE

We inevitably transform into optimistic people when we concentrate on all the positive aspects of our lives. Simply listing the good things that happen to us each day, small and big, for which we are grateful will boost our optimism and make us happier. Merely thinking about them will not help us make them come true; we need to write them down and act on them. We might encounter challenging circumstances on some days, or there might be roadblocks in our path, but every day has some positive aspects to it. For example, we can write down that we are grateful for our family, the food we eat, the water we drink, and so on.

COMMITTING TO CONTINUOUS IMPROVEMENT

The continuous improvement method emphasizes producing small progress over time rather than making significant improvements all at once. Improvements must be continually worked on in order to be maintained. Our pursuit of personal improvement never ends, and when we embrace it, we are much less likely to give up since we are constantly looking for the next challenge. For example, if you have a business, you will work on expanding it as much as you can by regularly developing and implementing better business ideas.

BEING HUMBLE

As already stated, we need to stay open to learning from more experienced people who have achieved the same goals we are pursuing so that we can follow in their steps. By the same token, we should stay humble because overconfidence can lead to arrogance. Take Koby Bryant, for example. Even when he became one of the best basketball players of all time, he still looked up to Michael Jordan, his coach, and others, who were able to teach him more things.

KEY TAKEAWAYS

- We all know how easy it is to fall into bad habits that we cannot get out of. Hence the need to establish new healthy habits in order to lead a better life.
- If we plan on forming a new habit, we should start with something small, an "atomic habit," as James Clear explains in his book. Nothing will stick to us if we start big because we can get overwhelmed and stop in the middle of the journey.
- According to Clear, there are also 4 steps in building healthy habits: cue, craving, response, and reward.
- No matter what your goals are, here are some healthy habits you should cultivate: not checking your phone first thing in the morning, keeping the promises you make to yourself, getting laser focus, overcoming your fears and taking risks, focusing on the results and ignoring the costs, writing down all the good things in your life, committing to continuous improvement, and not being arrogant.

12

ELIMINATING EXCUSES

"I attribute my success to this: - I never gave or took an excuse."-
Florence Nightingale

Making excuses is a typical human reaction because, as social creatures, we worry about what other people think of us and want to fit in. We create excuses and avoid responsibilities instead of dealing with difficult situations and emotions. Making excuses can make people feel relieved only for a moment since they have protected themselves from some discomfort (Robbins, 2022). However, over time, they might feel unfulfilled, anxious, or depressed because of this.

The hardest part about making excuses is that they frequently contain a bit of truth. Imagine that due to a car wreck, two roads were closed, causing you to miss the meeting that morning. It also may be true that on the evening your essay was due, the internet went out all of a sudden. Saying that you could have become more successful had your family supported you more sounds like a reasonable statement. There are lots of reasonable explanations for why success is very difficult to achieve. However, wouldn't you want to exchange each excuse for the chance to succeed? That is the problem with excuses. Despite how good they are, they show us that we did not do the things we set out to do. We must learn how to stop making them if we want to become self-disciplined and reach success later on.

WHY DO YOU MAKE EXCUSES?

We can make sure that we will always be in charge of our lives by understanding how to avoid making excuses. People typically make up excuses because they do not like a certain result in their lives. This might concern their health, income, family life, or careers. We have two options when asked why our lives are not the way we want them to be: We can give an excuse or we can take responsibility. Many people make the error of blaming their shortcomings on uncontrollable external factors for what happens. Although they may appear insignificant, excuses may seriously hinder our efforts to live the life of our dreams.

Let's say that your goal is to lose 30 pounds of weight in 3 months. At the end of 3 months, you weighed yourself and found out that you had only lost 10 pounds. As you consider what could have gone wrong, you think about all the cheat meals you had eaten when you should have been dieting. Moreover, you also remember the time you skipped your gym workout because you felt like you were too exhausted or busy. Instead of making excuses and actually accepting responsibility here, you give yourself the chance to do better in the future.

For example, if you recognize that you have failed to accomplish your weight loss target because you did not stick to the plan, what you can do is figure out how to follow it better. If you had followed all the steps in the plan and still did not reach the goal, then you should reconsider the plan you made. In this case, you might see if your plan was unrealistic for you to follow at the moment. You have two options in this scenario: You may either change your goal entirely or lengthen the time you give yourself to complete it. In either situation, you are fully aware of how to bring about the changes you desire in your life.

When we blame our failures on a scenario or situation that we cannot control, we will find ourselves waiting for the world to deliver us the life we want. Those who are aware of how excuses can hinder their chances of success will welcome the chance to accept responsibility for the things that happen in their lives (Griggs, 2022).

HOW TO ELIMINATE EXCUSES

UNDERSTANDING THE NEED TO LEAVE YOUR COMFORT ZONE

If we wish to eliminate excuses from our lives, we need to concentrate on the reasons why we desire a better life for ourselves. When hesitations enter our heads, we will begin to find excuses to maintain things just the way they are. Our desire to carry on is the furthest thing from our minds when we are in this situation.

Therefore, whatever excuse we may come up with is an effort to return to our comfortable environments. Yet the most dangerous thing about our comfort zone is precisely that it may feel so comfortable because of all the routines that we have gotten used to. The issue with keeping ourselves in our comfort zone is that it limits our ability to take risks and try new things, stretch our interests, and experience the improvements we wish to make.

AVOIDING OTHER EXCUSERS

When we begin moving outside our comfort zone, we will realize that a lot of people in our lives are also making excuses. If we analyze the conversations with them, we will find out how many times we would complain and make excuses for everything. Instead of engaging in these pointless conversations, we should spend our time doing something that is actually important.

Like us, these people do not know that they are making excuses; everybody must come to this conclusion on their own first before they can transform themselves. For example, when we talk to these people, we need to start a fresh conversation and be the ones to shift the topic so that we do not complain and whine about the things we can actually change. Eliminating our excuses will probably inspire others we care about to follow the same path.

KEEPING IN MIND YOUR REASONS TO PERSEVERE

We need to remind ourselves of our goals and work passionately toward them at all times if we want to step outside of our comfort zone and avoid making excuses. Each time we give in to excuses, we give ourselves a reason for accepting our lives as they are. There will constantly be an excuse to put something off until later, but we cannot let ourselves do this all the time. We have to ask ourselves, "How do I see myself changing if I achieve my goal? Will I be in a better position to look after my family and advocate for issues I care about?" No matter the reason, we have to realize that making excuses will prevent us from achieving our life goals.

NOT BLAMING OTHERS

People who make excuses frequently blame others for their situations. This way of thinking shows that we lack control over our life and rely too much on external factors rather than our efforts to influence them. As opposed to taking an active role in shaping our destiny, it makes us victims of life.

We all know a person who consistently finds someone else to blame for their problems and who is unhappy in many areas of their life. Maybe you are that person? Perhaps you like making excuses, whether you are blaming the place in which you live, your parents, or the condition of the world today. Many successful people have experienced hardships in their lives; some grew up poor, while others were forced to flee their homes, but they managed to rise above these adversities. It is essential that we take charge of our lives and understand that we are responsible for our future. In order to realize we are not alone and we are not victims, we can read and draw inspiration from others' success stories.

CONQUERING YOUR FEAR OF FAILURE

The ability to quit making excuses enables us to accept the fact that mistakes will occasionally happen. Most people make excuses for their inaction because they are afraid of failing. It is challenging to take a leap into doing a new thing. We find ourselves overwhelmed with thoughts about the worst-case scenario because we want to be safe (Brady, 2022).

As an example, if you are looking for a new job or to launch a business, your mind might be worried that you will lose your steady income. Your mind immediately starts coming up with all the reasons you need to stay at your current job when you begin to see yourself leaving. The promotion you did not get may make you question whether you ever wanted it. You might even ask yourself if dealing with more work and responsibilities is really worth all the hassle. You begin to consider yourself fortunate that you were not promoted once you realize that the higher income is not worth the stress of extra work.

You have come up with a number of excuses for keeping things as they are for a short period of time. The answer to all of these questions will be the same once you accept responsibility for the outcomes in your life. Even though you might not be certain of what is ahead of you, you are confident in your ability to handle the challenge. No matter the obstacle, you are confident that you will acquire the abilities required to overcome it.

KEY TAKEAWAYS

- As obvious as it may seem, we cannot allow ourselves to think that life is something that just happens to us because a lot of things in our lives are under our control.
- The first move in improving our lives is understanding how to quit making excuses since we are the ones who create them.
- An incredible thing will happen when we accept responsibility for our lives: We will begin to explore strategies to quit making excuses and have consistent self-discipline as a result.
- Tips on eliminating excuses: understanding the need to leave your comfort zone, avoiding other excusers, keeping in mind your reasons to persevere, not blaming others, and overcoming your fear of failure.

13

DOING THE THINGS UNSUCCESSFUL PEOPLE WON'T DO

"If you can get through doing things that you hate to do, on the other side is greatness."- David Goggins

This sounds like an old cliché but it is true; everybody wants to be successful, yet only a limited number of people actually get to the point where they can enjoy both their professional and personal achievements, no matter how small. How do we stay away from the dangers and bad habits that most unsuccessful people engage in? We can do this by doing all the things that unsuccessful people won't do. Precisely because it is so

127

easy to pass up opportunities, we need to learn how to take more action in our lives because successful people are more willing to move forward. Here are some of the activities that successful people need to do.

TAKING MORE RISKS

Successful people have a very different attitude than unsuccessful ones, as can be seen by observing their behavior. A willingness to take risks is one of the key traits separating successful and unsuccessful people. Let's say you are interested in the stock market and want to invest someday. However, you are scared that you may not be able to get any profit if your calculation is wrong. Successful people will try their best to learn all about the stock market and take the risk of losing money. Even if they fail the first time, they can still learn from their mistakes and try another time.

As pointed out in the previous chapter, doing only what feels comfortable will not benefit us in the long run. We cannot avoid taking risks in life, so we might as well embrace challenges, thinking of them as opportunities to practice self-discipline and thereby to learn and grow. If we can accomplish a difficult task, we will gain the confidence necessary to take on others.

DEALING WITH A CHALLENGE, NO MATTER HOW DIFFICULT

Our brains thrive on a challenge, but only when it is presented in the correct way. If something is too simple, our minds become bored and switch to a different thing. If it is too difficult, we instantly lose interest and shift to something else. Taking on challenges involves more than just being willing to have uncomfortable discussions, recognizing failure as a necessary part of the process, and remaining true to our vision. Additionally, it involves continually repeating the steps, despite how boring and challenging they may get.

For example, talent alone is insufficient in order to become a great runner. Having the right body is also not enough here. A runner must increase their endurance over longer distances by constantly performing a ton of exercises even though these might feel like an endless stretch of roads in the beginning. A great runner is created over time because they are willing to go through difficult and boring challenges.

FOCUSING ON YOUR GOALS DAILY

Envisaging success is another trait of successful people. For example, Vanessa has been writing down her goals as soon as she wakes up every morning for years. In her experience, no matter how ridiculous the goal is, if she can maintain her concentration, she will succeed in achieving it. She believes that when she has a clear sense of her unfulfilled goals, they are more likely to become a reality. We can try to do the same as Vanessa and focus on our success by making it clear in our minds. Unsuccessful people do not seem to be in control of what they concentrate on; they tend to let anything wander into their thoughts and environments. Despite how big or insignificant our goals are, we all have the chance to accomplish them every day.

GETTING UP EARLY

A lot of unsuccessful people refuse to get up early in the morning or even get out of bed. In order to have more time to reach our goals, we need to push ourselves to wake up early. Approximately half of the self-made billionaires rose a minimum of three hours before their workday officially began (Ward, 2017). Most of them work on personal projects in their spare time, create plans for their days, or schedule workouts. Why do they do this, and why do we need to follow this habit? We will be able to take back control of our lives by waking at 5 a.m. and tackling the top three tasks we want to complete for the day. As a result, we feel more confident in what we do and take charge of our lives too.

SPENDING TIME WITH THOSE WHO INSPIRE YOU

As mentioned in the previous chapters, spending time with those who inspire you is a must if you want to be successful. We are only as successful as the people we hang around with the most. We should not worry if we do not yet have highly driven individuals in our personal network. A lot of successful businessmen spend their free time volunteering, which is a fantastic way to connect with other inspiring, driven people (Imafidon, 2022). Moreover, we can also join communities for people with similar hobbies or careers and then communicate with them in order to establish relationships. We also have to choose whom we spend time with carefully. Additionally, successful people make it a point to limit their contact with toxic and negative individuals.

BEING CAUTIOUSLY OPTIMISTIC

Wherever possible, successful people focus their attention on the positive side of things, yet not blindly. Having an optimistic attitude enables us to see possibilities and alternatives that we otherwise would not, while accepting that we cannot always predict or control the future. Still, we must have faith that we can cope with the obstacles that we are likely to encounter along the way; otherwise, we will either give up before the trip is over or fail in our journey.

Hence the need to become good thinkers so that we can find solutions whenever something negative comes our way. One of the most important tools for a successful individual is critical thinking. Problem-solvers are constantly coming up with new ideas and looking toward the future. For example, if you have just been laid off, what are you going to do? Keeping a positive attitude does not mean that you can just sit around and wait for opportunities to come to you. You will need to take action. Perhaps this is your chance to implement the business idea that you have been putting off. You have to believe that there are opportunities out there and be willing to go after them.

READING BOOKS

Unsuccessful people do not care about gaining new knowledge and understanding others' perspectives. If we want to become successful, we need to expand our horizons by reading books in a variety of genres, such as biography, history, self-help, and fiction. Reading for pleasure can also advance our professional careers (Ward, 2016). Warren Buffet, a renowned investor and self-made billionaire, claims that reading is his most important habit (Ward, 2017). After reading a book, we also need to apply the knowledge we have learned in real life, or it will be useless. For instance, if you have just read a self-help book on quitting procrastination, you have to start practicing the tips mentioned there. If not, you will never be able to quit procrastination as you intend to do.

SETTING BOUNDARIES

Successful people set not only specific goals but also clear boundaries in pursuit of those goals. Thus, if you work in the business world, you need to realize that not all business ideas are good, and not all partnerships are advantageous for you. Successful businessmen are aware that they cannot accept every proposal or collaborate with everybody. Oftentimes we have to put our needs first, taking a little break and saying no to more hours of work. It might feel like we are not working hard enough, but we all need time for ourselves and our loved ones.

KEY TAKEAWAYS

- What sets successful and unsuccessful people apart? It is all about taking action and moving forward with our plans, in spite of obstacles or fear of failure.
- A successful person demonstrates the persistence and commitment necessary for success. They practice self-discipline, are determined to succeed, and put in a lot of effort. People who are successful are also tireless in these pursuits.
- Things unsuccessful people won't do: taking more risks, dealing with a challenge, focusing on goals daily, getting up early, spending time with those who inspire you, being cautiously optimistic, reading books, and setting boundaries.

14

PLANNING YOUR DAY BY CREATING A TO-DO LIST

"Make a damn schedule."- Jordan Person

It is often said that the best, if not the only way, to control the future is to plan for it. Establishing a schedule of activities we wish to complete each day allows us to stay productive and organized. When people implement such plans into their routines, the majority of them notice significant advantages in their lives. Planning your day is best done the night prior or first thing each morning. You can choose the time depending on what works for you best.

THE ADVANTAGES OF PLANNING YOUR DAY

FREEING UP MORE TIME IN YOUR DAY

Most people do not even consider planning their days because they genuinely believe that doing so will limit their freedom. They claim that planning their time reduces their flexibility. They believe it will drain the day's excitement and ruin their "young, wild, and free" mentality (Canelas, 2021). Consider, however, consider the possibility–and consequences–of a missed deadline or a forgotten task.

We outline our future success when we start each day with a clear plan. We possess the freedom to set aside time for work, fun, extracurricular activities, and side hobbies. We are able to create the freedom we desire instead of waiting for it to come. If we feel like working additional hours on particular days, we can plan those times in advance. Alternatively, if we feel like staying away from work, either to relax or spend time with the family, we can take a day off as well.

In my case, once I started doing daily planning, I had the opportunity to read books, keep a journal, travel, spend quality time with my loved ones, and learn new things. It was not a matter of having the time anymore; it was a matter of making the time.

BECOMING MORE PRODUCTIVE AND LESS BUSY

As an example, Matthew has never tried to plan his working days before, and as a result, he never knows where to start doing his tasks. When his work is not busy and there is not much to do, he is fine. However, when his boss gives him a lot of tasks at once, he becomes very overwhelmed and ends up wasting time on unnecessary things—until one day, when his coworker suggests that he starts planning his day. Matthew finally does so and after a while, he realizes that everything becomes so organized that he is no longer wasting time on pointless activities. While time-filler activities occupy our time for their own sake without producing anything, time-feeder activities fill it with progress and accomplishments (Canelas, 2022). Planning our day also increases our productive hours as opposed to merely working more hours. When we make a plan for the day, we intentionally choose whether to be busy or productive with our time. We can start by figuring out what contributes most to the things we are working on, followed by developing a plan, putting it into action, and managing our productive time.

FEELING MORE EXCITED

When we plan our day, we will feel more excited to go through it. We are all aware of the excitement that comes with organizing our next vacations; this excitement typically matches that of actually going on holiday. The process of picturing and writing out a plan offers us something to hold on to, even when that thing is repetitive. For example, you have a blog where you like to write and post different articles about celebrities. Choosing whom to focus on next adds to the excitement of writing your posts. You know you do this every week, but because your focus varies, you will still be enthusiastic about this activity each time.

ENHANCING YOUR FOCUS

We all have been through those awful mornings when nothing makes sense. We are unsure of our responsibilities, so we lack focus as we move from task to task since there is no plan to guide us. Those days, which I refer to as trashy days, have that feeling. On the other hand, when our day is planned out in advance, we are less inclined to fall victim to distractions or lose time wondering what we need to do next. With a plan in place, it will be easier to navigate the day, without doubts or uncertainties. A plan gives us direction and purpose, focusing our attention on our long-term goal and the tasks at hand.

GETTING MORE QUALITY SLEEP

Oskar has been having a hard time sleeping during the night. He has a big project coming up at work and he is not sure where to begin or how to do it well. He feels that the project is so overwhelming that it has taken over his sleeping hours. An overactive mind full of racing thoughts is one of the most typical causes of insomnia. It is difficult to get quality sleep and stay asleep if we cannot stop thinking and worrying. All humans experience fears and anxieties about the future, but there are ways to minimize the stress of such thoughts. While writing them down can be therapeutic, it is planning that genuinely frees us from these worries. Making plans for the following day in the evening can help us get better quality sleep and feel more relaxed (Marvin, 2022).

MEETING YOUR DEADLINES BY SCAFFOLDING YOUR PROJECTS

We can more easily meet deadlines when we plan our day. Doing so may help us break our big projects into small tasks so that we can establish a timeline to make sure that we complete them by a specific time or date. We will also be able to keep track of important deadlines and remind ourselves about them by reviewing the schedule every day. This practice also enables us to modify our schedule as we go. For example, your team is tasked by your company to create a new logo for them. This is a big project, so when you plan your day, you need to divide it into manageable tasks. You can say that on the first day you will brainstorm ideas with your team, on the second day you will create the design, and so forth.

HAVING LESS STRESS

Lack of organization causes high levels of stress that are detrimental to our health, both physical and mental, thus preventing us from producing quality work. We can all draw up a list of goals, activities, and tasks that are realistic and thus attainable. However, without a guide to follow, we will probably struggle or simply give up. One advantage of planning our day is stress reduction. For example, if you want to quit your current job and get a new one, the steps to get a new job would be to update your resume, search for job vacancies, and apply to different companies. Once you get accepted to a new job, your next step would be to submit your resignation letter, wait for the two-week notice, and then finally start your new job. When we have outlined the ways to get there, we will worry less about the outcome. Even though the plan might not always yield the best or desired outcome, at least we have a strong starting point. With a set strategy, we will be able to accomplish far more with a lot less stress.

HOW TO CREATE A TO-DO LIST

A to-do list is a collection of things that we need to get done within a certain time frame, such as a day, a week, or even only a part of the day (Kiander, 2022). These lists, which frequently contain manageable activities, encourage productivity and prevent procrastination. There are often two styles for to-do lists: either we place the most important things at the top and the least significant ones at the bottom, or we arrange the activities so that they progress from easily achievable to more difficult. Staying organized and setting reminders to become much easier as a result. So how do you create a to-do list? Here are some steps.

Firstly, you should not create the list in a hurry; instead, take your time, giving yourself at least 15 minutes. If necessary, find a quiet place, whether inside or outside our house, so that you can carefully analyze your tasks before adding them to the to-do list. Secondly, write tasks and not goals. The latter should be on a different list. While tasks might help us move toward our goals, goals are bigger objectives that we cannot accomplish in a single day. For example, if your goal is to learn to speak Spanish, you can break it down into a task by writing "see a movie in Spanish" or "read a Spanish book for 20 minutes."

Thirdly, keep your to-do lists brief so that they can be read quickly to determine what needs to be done next. To this end, look for keywords identifying the relevant tasks. If let's say, you intend to clean up your house, you might jot down something short, like "clean house," rather than a long sentence.

Lastly, prioritize your tasks. It is difficult to know the exact number of tasks we should have on our daily to-do list. Depending on our circumstances, anything between 5 and 10 activities should be sufficient for the day. We should recognize that some tasks can be completed quickly, making it simpler to add more and organize our activities on certain days.

TIPS ON PLANNING YOUR DAY

When attempting to create a plan for our day, there are several things we can do to increase its effectiveness. Here are some tips we can utilize in order to create a good to-do list.

USING A PLANNING TOOL

Organizing our day will be much easier with a planning tool. An actual paper planner, a smartphone app, or software applications are all examples of planning tools. If we create our to-do list in the same place each day, we will always know where to find it. It will also become easier to review past plans to include relevant information for that day. Pick a planning tool that fits your needs the best.

CREATING CATEGORIES FOR YOUR TASKS

We can try categorizing our tasks for better organization within our daily agenda. We may analyze our most frequent tasks, then categorize them into groups based on similarity. For instance, we can create sections for meetings, calls and emails, work projects, and personal matters. We will be able to see more clearly the kind of tasks we have for the day by establishing categories.

LEAVING SPACE FOR ADJUSTMENTS

It can be helpful to create your to-do list while keeping in mind that changes might be necessary due to unforeseen circumstances. For instance, if we know that we have a task that needs to be completed at the end of the day, we can try to get it done one hour earlier. This will give us the time to complete our tasks before something unpredictable occurs during the day. In order to create this extra time in our daily plan, we can either allow ourselves more time than we estimate for more difficult tasks or set aside some free time.

UPDATING YOUR PLANS DURING THE DAY

It would be ideal if we were able to stick to our schedule every day exactly as it was intended. However, unpredictable circumstances sometimes may occur, and they occasionally make finishing a task take longer or shorter than expected. It is a good idea to modify our daily schedule during the day to get the most out of it. For instance, if we complete a task early, we can reschedule, or even get started on, other tasks that were set for later in the day.

REVIEWING YOUR PROGRESS AT THE END OF EACH DAY

Make a habit of reviewing your to-do list each night, looking very closely for any tasks you were not able to finish that day. These things can be included in your plan for the following day to help you remember to finish them. check whether certain tasks took you longer or shorter than intended when reviewing your progress for the day so that you can make future plans that are more accurate. For instance, if you find that you have often finished a task ahead of schedule, you can allocate less time when you need to do that task again.

KEY TAKEAWAYS

- When we have so many things to do, it can get very overwhelming when we are not sure where to start doing our tasks. Hence it is very important for us to plan our day by creating a to-do list.
- Creating a to-do list will enable us to get more freedom in our day, become more productive and less busy, feel more excited, enhance our focus, get more quality sleep, meet our deadlines, scaffold big projects, and have less stress.
- In order to get through our day much more easier, we need to take our time in making the to-do list, putting tasks, not goals on it, setting our priorities, and leaving room for the unexpected.
- Some important tips for planning our day so that it can be effective and we can turn it into our new habit are as follows: using a planning tool, creating categories for our tasks, updating our plans during the day, and reviewing our progress at the end of each day.

15

FINDING AN ACCOUNTABILITY PARTNER

"Your accountability partner keeps you on track and moving forward in all aspects of your development."- Mike Staver

WHAT EXACTLY IS ACCOUNTABILITY AND WHY DOES IT MATTER?

Taking accountability means recognizing that you are the only one who is responsible for your success. It involves taking responsibility for your actions and for pursuing attainable, realistic goals for success. Accountability is the measurement we use to assess every action's influence and effect as well as determine whether it will move us closer or further away from our end goals (Finkelstein, 2020). Simply put, accountability means doing what you say you will do. For example, let's imagine that you say you are going to open up a new business. If you hold yourself accountable for that decision, you will definitely start doing the things needed to launch the business idea.

Accountability is crucial in every undertaking. It ensures that we thoroughly analyze our decisions and weigh the results of each action against the goal we intend to accomplish. Accountability assists us not just in overcoming uncertainty but also in maintaining our motivation and overcoming negative views, feelings, and behavior patterns (Braun, 2022). However, if we often struggle to hold ourselves accountable or if we are unsure of how to begin practicing self-accountability, then we might benefit from having an accountability partner to guide us. Keep in mind that having an accountability partner is different from having a mentor.

WHY DO YOU NEED AN ACCOUNTABILITY PARTNER?

We have already emphasized, in Chapter 9, the benefits of surrounding yourself with successful people, but the ideal companion for your self-exploratory journey toward accountability is an accountability partner (Finkelstein, 2022). That person might be a supportive friend, family member, colleague, or even an outsider–a knowledgeable and caring individual who can help you maintain focus and motivation while you're working toward your goals, and who can also help you identify your strengths and weaknesses. The more specific benefits of having an accountability partner are described below.

OFFERING GUIDANCE AND ADVICE

Our accountability partners can help us evaluate our success because they are unbiased witnesses of our journey. They can also guide us in determining our strengths and shortcomings. They will identify areas that need more focus and attention so that we can improve them. For instance, if you desire to get promoted at your workplace, an accountability partner can help tell you which skills to improve or which habits to get rid of. If you have a bad habit of showing up late to work, your accountability partner will hold you accountable for this behavior and ask you to change in order to get the promotion. In doing so, we will be able to gain a deeper insight into our behavior, ideas, and feelings.

HELPING YOU STAY ON TRACK

An accountability partner, who genuinely cares about our goals and supports them, might assist in helping us identify the moments when we start to lose focus. By reminding us of the advantages of reaching our goals, they can help us to get back on track and serve as a constant source of inspiration and encouragement. They also help in keeping our energy and willpower–indeed, our discipline–strong.

Let's say you plan to expand your business to another country, but you come up against so many hurdles that you end up putting it off. In this scenario, an accountability partner would be there to remind you about your goal and encourage you to stick to your plan. Telling yourself "I have plenty of time" or "I can do it whenever I want" will never help you grow. This kind of attitude will never be enough in getting you to follow through on your goals because you will keep thinking that there is always tomorrow to take action.

HELPING YOU PUSH YOUR LIMITS

We will be able to test our skills and identify areas where more substantial improvement can be made with the assistance of an accountability partner. We can then aim higher and set more important goals. For example, you are not sure that you can get promoted at work because you think that your public speaking and leadership abilities are lacking. An accountability partner will be the one to push you to improve these skills so that you can get a better position at work. In general, accountability allows us to discover and make the most of our abilities, but sometimes we all need a nudge in the right direction or a reminder of what we are truly capable of. We cannot always get to a better place if we go and do it alone. The journey becomes a more meaningful experience with others by our side.

SHARING IN OUR HAPPINESS AND SUCCESS

The ideal person with whom to share our happiness and success in our accomplishments is an accountability partner. Our accountability partners can help us gain a fresh perspective on all the goals we have achieved and set new ones, thus boosting our self-confidence and motivating us to excel at what we are doing. When we collaborate and build on each other's strengths while recognizing our shortcomings, we may help each other succeed and grow. Once we have achieved our goals, we can then share our happiness and victories with them.

HOW TO DISCOVER THE RIGHT ACCOUNTABILITY PARTNER

Choosing and discovering an accountability partner can be challenging because we are looking for someone who

- is pursuing goals that match with yours
- assumes responsibility for those goals as well
- is at ease discussing sensitive information with you and you with them
- uses similar methods of communication, such as email, text messages, phone calls, video calls, or in-person.

Finding someone who meets our criteria can seem like finding a needle in a haystack, but we can increase our chances if we make a conscious effort to do so.

MAKING A LIST

The first step in finding an accountability partner is to compile a list of people who we already know might be a good fit, starting with our current circle of friends, family members, or coworkers. We should reach out to them, explain our goals briefly, and ask whether they would be keen to take on the challenge with us.

It would help to give any networking groups we belong to some consideration as well. Do we have any connections with somebody who we think may be a good match? We do not have to limit our quest to offline networking groups, of course, as we can also look for an online accountability partner. We can post information about our attempts in groups on Twitter or LinkedIn. A person who would love to collaborate with us might respond to our posts or message us privately.

LOOKING FOR VALUES THAT MATCH

We should think about our prospective accountability partner very carefully, choosing somebody whose values and viewpoints align with ours so that we can get the most out of our collaboration. For instance, you want to open up a new business. If you place a high value on servicing customers, and your partner cares more about earnings at the expense of clients, your relationship will not work. If your values clash with theirs, you won't be able to support each other. You need to research that person's background and credentials before agreeing to enter into an accountability relationship with them. Check their posts on social media, blogs, and websites. Do they frequently voice complaints about their clients? Do they regularly spread negative stories? When their name appears in your news stream, do you feel uncomfortable? All of these red flags should tell you that you will not get along with this person. When we are tempted to compromise our values and morals, a trustworthy accountability partner can be a big help.

KEEPING IT SHORT-TERM

We should keep things casual in the beginning when we discover somebody who we believe would be a suitable accountability partner. We should agree to a short trial period of between one to three months. Following this period, we can review our partnership and determine whether to keep it going. This allows us and our partners the chance to discuss our basic values, objectives, and principles. We must take our time and not rush our first meeting with our accountability partners because getting to know them can be exciting.

KEY TAKEAWAYS

- An accountability partner is a great addition to our accountability journey because they can offer guidance and advice, help us stay on track, and push our limits, while also sharing in our happiness and success.
- We have to also keep in mind that we need to be careful while choosing our accountability partners because the wrong person might seriously hinder our success while the right person can greatly help in achieving our goals.
- Things to pay attention to while choosing an accountability partner: They must be pursuing goals that match with yours, want responsibility for those goals as well, are at ease discussing sensitive information with you and you with them, and use similar methods of communication.

16

VISUALIZING YOUR SUCCESS

"Imagination is everything. It is the preview of life's coming attractions"- Albert Einstein

A lot of high achievers make effective use of the powers of visualization to plan, carry out, actualize, and accomplish their goals one small step at a time. While the rest of us may not be aware of or know how to use it, we all possess the power to visualize and achieve our goals. We benefit from visualizing because it allows us to establish important habits for success. Without it, we will not be able to continue moving toward our bigger life goals.

WHAT DOES VISUALIZING YOUR SUCCESS MEAN?

When we think about visualizing our success, we have two things in mind: visualization and success. So what exactly is visualization? It is the practice of constantly envisioning future goals as though they were already realized today. If we equate success with achieving these goals, then we can say that visualizing our success entails having vivid dreams and convincing our subconscious to embrace the way of life we associate with that success (Ngako, 2022). It is like giving ourselves the go-ahead to fulfill all of our lifelong goals and become whatever we ever wanted in life.

THE IMPORTANCE AND BENEFITS OF VISUALIZATION

We live in a world shaped by digital technologies that have opened new doors for business companies. Remote work is now accessible at the press of a button, but digital distractions often cause us to get sidetracked. Instead of trying to master multitasking, we need to take a step back and concentrate on the things that are most important to us. By utilizing the technique of visualization, we will be able to establish the mindset necessary to turn our future goals into reality.

In creative visualization, we can train our brains to concentrate on what is most important to us and to practice the process of selective attention. Have you ever purchased a car only to discover that everyone else appears to be using the same model? We see what we decide to pay attention to, and this is what selective attention means (Moe, 2021). Our chances of making a goal a reality increase the more we concentrate on it and work toward it.

By visualizing our success, we take control of our lives and ensure that it is in line with our long-term goals. The process also allows us to develop our ideas and see what is achievable. Additionally, visualization helps us remain aware of who we are as people and our life goals. Life becomes easier when we envisage our future as our present reality. Now that we understand why visualizing our success is important, let's take a closer look at the specific benefits we can reap from it.

INCREASING POSITIVE THOUGHTS

During the day, we will have a constant internal dialogue. Here, we need to be friends with ourselves and not destructive opponents, so we have to be conscious of our thoughts and pick them wisely. For example, if you are currently looking for a job, instead of thinking that you will fail and be unemployed forever, you need to visualize how you get a job and actually do the job in your mind. We will start attracting great results into our lives by thinking more positively today. The first day will not give us any noticeable changes, but reinforcement works like planting seeds. We will start to feel happier right away, and as time passes, things in our lives will start to change for the better.

DEFINING WHAT YOU WANT

By visualizing our success, we will be able to learn to shift our focus from what we do not want to what we do want to accomplish. We can let go of all the negative emotions and focus instead on the actions that will help us reach our own goals. For instance, if your goal is to buy a new car by this year, instead of thinking that you will not be able to save enough money, you should visualize yourself driving that car you want. In this way, you will be sure of what you want and then take the necessary steps in order to achieve that. Once your goal has been defined, you can then keep doing regular visualization exercises. The more specific our visualization, the more attainable our goals will seem to us.

IMPROVING MOTIVATION

Motivational visualization includes visualizing achieving our ultimate success and the emotions that go along with it. All our senses should be stimulated, and we should become so involved in a mental image that it feels real to us. For example, if your goal is to pass all of your exams, you can visualize it in your mind as if you have accomplished it. In this way, you will feel more motivated to study more in order to achieve this goal because you feel excited about the success that will come up in the future. The more you are accustomed to feeling successful, the more motivated you will be to complete your task, and the more likely you will be to succeed.

TIPS ON VISUALIZING YOUR SUCCESS

THINKING ABOUT YOURSELF GETTING WHAT YOU WANT IN LIFE

We can start off by focusing on the positive and allowing ourselves to believe that we will achieve our goals. It seems obvious, but the truth is that if we think we cannot do something, we will never succeed. Self-doubts can set us up for failure, but visualization helps to dispel them, thus fostering a growth mindset. That is all there is to it: visualizing ourselves achieving our objectives.

For example, we can picture ourselves taking a giant step to cross a fictional finish line or shaking the CEO's hands. The idea is to imprint that image in our minds. Then, it will be much easier to cultivate a positive attitude and feel confident in our ability to succeed. Nothing can stop us if we learn to visualize our success as if it has already happened. In addition, not even procrastination, which frequently interferes with our goals, can stop us here. To visualize achieving our goals is to affirm our commitment to them.

MAKING A VISION BOARD

The tip above concentrates on traditional methods of visualization through which a situation is internally visualized. However, some people have aphantasia, which prevents them from making up mental images (Ngako, 2022). We can alternatively make a vision board if we fall into this category or like to work with things that are concrete. Simply put, a vision board is a compilation of pictures and images that serve as a constant reminder of our own goals. Keeping a visual board somewhere close to your workspace will ensure that we stay on track—and true to our vision.

For example, if you want to lose weight, you can make a vision board with pictures of the things you wish to accomplish over time. You should not place your vision board too far away from where you can frequently view it. As a note, anything that can be measured can be monitored and improved upon.

PICTURING A HAPPY PLACE

Success may *look* different to different people, but it evokes the same feeling of contentment that you experience when you are, whether literally or metaphorically, in a happy place. When you struggle to finish a project and feel exhausted or overwhelmed, it helps to go to your happy place—a beach, an art exhibit, a rock concert, or anywhere you can unwind or recharge your batteries. Once you feel calm and relaxed, that place becomes a state of mind that you long to experience again and again.

EXPLORING POSSIBLE SOLUTIONS

In most instances, it is beneficial to think back on our visualization methods as a way of preparing for situations that might arise in the future. If the situation is uncertain or unpleasant, we can use this strategy. A good illustration is when we prepare to sit down with our supervisors and have a challenging discussion with them. If we plan ahead and visualize them, we will be aware of potential conversation topics and questions our supervisors might bring up. When we explore potential outcomes, the result frequently works in our favor. Furthermore, anticipating a possible problem allows us to better handle it as it occurs.

PLACING YOURSELF IN ANOTHER PERSON'S SHOES

There is a good chance that we can think of someone who, in the past, faced a similar obstacle to the one we are presently experiencing. We can imagine ourselves in their position right now. By doing so, we will be able to relate to the person's best or worst traits. When faced with an issue, we will come up with potential solutions to it. In order to visualize our success, it is essential to put ourselves in the other person's shoes. In that scenario, we should select a role model we admire and research the steps they took to achieve their success.

CREATING A NOTECARD

A notecard is a fantastic tool for detailing our success goals, keeping us in check, and reminding us of our daily tasks and long-term goals. Articulating our goals with conviction and intention can bring us closer to making them a reality. For instance, instead of something like, "My goal is to get a job as a software engineer by applying to various job vacancies," we need to be more specific: "I will get a new job as a software engineer by taking courses to improve skills in software development, creating a great resume, and then applying to good companies that are looking for a new software engineer." The clearer our intentions, the more inclined we will be to act upon them. Like the vision board, a notecard should be kept in a visible place, close at hand, so that we can refer to it frequently.

ADDING POSITIVE ENERGY TO YOUR VISUALIZATION

When we are feeling down, positive thinking can lift our spirits and lower our stress levels. Thus, we must think positively whenever we build our visualizations. Any negative thoughts we have should be met—so that they can be ultimately offset—by an equal amount of positive ones. We should avoid telling ourselves, "This goal seems too impossible to reach; I will never be able to accomplish it," for instance, and instead train our minds to reject these self-doubts with the belief that no matter the challenges we might face along the way, we can still succeed if we keep trying. A dose of optimism, however small, is all we need to start exploring the power of positive thinking.

KEY TAKEAWAYS

- High achievers frequently employ visualization strategies to accomplish their goals and achieve success.
- By visualizing our success, we will develop a positive attitude, motivate ourselves better, and clarify what we desire. Doing so will allow us to confront the obstacles that come our way head-on and overcome them.
- Some tips on visualizing your success: imagining yourself getting what you want in life, making a vision board, picturing a happy place, exploring possible solutions, placing yourself in another person's shoes, creating a notecard, and adding positive energy to your visualization.
- Naturally, visualizing our success becomes easier the more we practice it. That being said, the moment to begin practicing it is now.

17

FINDING YOUR WHY AND FOCUSING ON IT AS OFTEN AS POSSIBLE

"When something is important enough, you do it even if the odds are not in your favor."- Elon Musk

If we want to have consistent self-discipline, we would have to find real reasons and purposes for doing what we need to do. If we have ever had to deal with a serious crisis in our lives, we will have experienced the power of purpose to draw on energies, persistence, and bravery we probably were not even aware we possessed. Our mission was very clear and compelling. We had a laser-like focus. Our potential was also tapped. When we have a clear sense of purpose, we will be able to concentrate our efforts on the things that matter most, which drives us to take chances and move forward in spite of difficulties or challenges.

Imagine, for example, that you are attending a business meeting, or a school event when you receive a call that a member of your family has been severely injured in an accident and taken to the hospital. You will feel the urgent, desperate need to reach out to your loved one. Nothing else would concern you. Nobody and nothing could get in your way as you rushed to see your loved one. You'd be committed to doing whatever it takes for a strong reason. Thus, if getting there was the only challenge because you did not own a car, you might decide to run or perhaps even carjack one in order to go see your family member. If, when you arrived at the hospital, a security guard tried to stop you, would you give in and leave? Of course not. You would not act that way. You would do anything to enter the hospital room where your loved one was in.

Our lack of strong reasons for going after what we desire to accomplish is the root of all the excuses and foolish things we say and do that slow us back. In order to get what we desire we must be desperate. If we are not, we will fall into the 'I will like this or that" category of individuals who never get to experience the satisfaction of accomplishing their goals because they are not hungry or desperate for them. They lack compelling reasons to accomplish their life goals.

THE ADVANTAGES OF FINDING YOUR WHY

Humans have more desires in life than their animal counterparts, who are just motivated by the need to survive. We might experience discouragement, distraction, and hopelessness if we do not have an answer to the question, "survival for the purpose of what?" (Warrell, 2013). Understanding your why is a crucial first step in finding out how to accomplish the goals that motivate you and build a life you enjoy living rather than one you are just trying to survive. In fact, you will not have the ability to take the risks necessary to develop in life, keep going when things get tough, or radically change your life's trajectory until you first understand why you are doing what you are doing.

People who are aware of their life's purpose typically lead more fulfilling lives than those who are not. Because we are aware of who we are, where we have come from, and where we are going, we tend to live our day to the fullest. What, then, are some other advantages of knowing your why?

First, it gives meaning to our life. Once we know it, we will be able to get closer to our goals with each step we take and every bit of effort we put forth. When actions are taken with a clear purpose and objective in mind, they become significantly easier to complete.

Second, it establishes a value system. Knowing our why also enables us to identify and establish a set of basic values that will direct us in the years to come. For example, if you know that your purpose in life is to become a famous actor in Hollywood, you will focus on reaching it and taking the necessary steps in order to accomplish it. You do not have to waste time and effort every day attempting to determine whether what you are doing is actually right or worthwhile. You will know that you are on the right path if it fits your purpose. That greatly boosts your confidence in your actions.

Third, it boosts your self-esteem. We will have a great deal of pride in what we accomplish when we find our why and are striving toward something important. Our self-worth and sense of value will also grow with every day that goes by and with each little move we take in the right direction. We should use that feeling to motivate ourselves to face the obstacles that may arise in the future.

Lastly, it helps to improve your health, both physical and mental. Living a purpose-driven life can prevent depression and reduce the risk of stroke and cardiovascular disease (Willis, 2022). Indeed, finding meaning and purpose in our daily activities is one of the best methods to combat anxiety and stress (Morin, 2022).

TIPS ON FINDING YOUR WHY

KNOWING WHAT MAKES YOU FEEL ALIVE

We feel more alive when we are working toward goals that inspire us. These have to do with more than going on our dream vacation or watching our favorite football team play and win their game. As such, these goals reflect a deeper why, one that connects us with others and attaches us to something that is greater than ourselves. When we follow our passion, we focus on things that ignite that passion, but real fulfillment comes from the impact we have and the difference we make in the world around us.

We do not need to say right now that we wish to create the next Apple product, find a solution to the world's energy issues, or find a cure for cancer. Although we might in the future, this is about us getting involved with a cause that is both greater than ourselves and consistent with our values.

FIGURING OUT YOUR NATURAL TALENT

What are the things you have always excelled at and occasionally question why others find them so difficult? In the middle of complexity, are you able to spot patterns and potentials? Are you naturally inclined at thinking outside the box and being creative? Are you particularly skilled at completing tasks with such accuracy that other people find it boring? Are you great at details? Or are you an exceptionally talented networker, organizer, critical thinker, technologist, negotiator, or agent of change? Of course, we can also be skilled at something we do not feel particularly passionate about. However, as I have learned through experience, we rarely aim for goals that we lack the natural talent to accomplish.

ASKING FOR FEEDBACK

Oftentimes it might be challenging to identify the things we are enthusiastic and passionate about. After all, we likely have a wide range of interests, and it is possible that some of them have become so ingrained in our lives that we are unaware of their significance. Luckily, someone else may be able to provide some light on the situation. Without ever realizing it, there is a strong chance that we are already sharing our passions and purposes with the people around us.

We can decide to reach out to people and discover what they think of us or whom we remind them of. If someone compliments us or makes a comment about us, we should also try to pay attention to it. We can write down these observations and look for patterns in them. Whether others describe us as brilliant entertainers or admire us for assisting the elderly, hearing what these people think of us may reaffirm to us the passions we have already been pursuing.

ENGAGING IN CONVERSATIONS WITH NEW PEOPLE

While waiting for a friend at a restaurant or while riding public transportation by ourselves, it is very easy to turn to our smartphones and explore social media. We should try to suppress that urge and instead spend some time interacting with those around us. We can try to find out what they enjoy doing for entertainment or if they are working on any tasks. We can also ask them about any groups they are a part of or if they have a favorite charity they prefer to donate to.

Although starting to talk to individuals outside of our personal social circles might feel unpleasant at first, doing so can open our eyes to pursuits, issues, or employment opportunities that we were previously unaware of. Through this, we may be able to come upon unique activities to pursue or new destinations to explore, which will further assist us in discovering our why.

TURNING YOUR SUFFERING INTO PURPOSE

We all have our struggles and face different obstacles in life. When attempting to deal with a significant life change, a lot of people seek assistance from others. Some people later discover their calling by guiding those going through the same difficulties they did. Some people decide to work with and help people directly, as social workers, for instance. Other people choose to influence the lives of others through creating art and making music. Some others become life coaches, motivational speakers, or teachers to inspire others to better their lives and those of future generations.

It is really up to us how we want to turn our suffering into something positive.

SUPPORTING A CAUSE YOU CARE ABOUT

A lot of people care about issues related to local, national, or global injustices and want to find solutions to them. What worries or bothers you in the world today? What do you feel strongly about? If solving problems like economic inequality, animal cruelty, racial and gender violence, global warming, or the mental health crisis is too daunting, remember that there are other causes out there—and organizations devoted to them—that could use our support. If the thought of elderly people spending the holidays by themselves makes us sad, or if we believe that drug users need more chances for recovery, then our purpose should be clear. As long as the cause is dear to our hearts, we can provide time, cash, or both.

SETTING ASIDE TIME FOR SELF-CARE

Self-care can take many different forms, and only we can define what that means for ourselves. Maybe we enjoy taking walks in the woods, practicing breathing techniques, or expressing our feelings in a journal. Why is self-care so crucial to practice? Because our minds are most productive and creative when they are comfortable and calm. When we compete with ourselves, we will never be able to accomplish anything or be of service to others. Have you ever realized that when you are showering, you discover a lot of great ideas? This is because when we let ideas come to us naturally rather than forcing them, our minds are more flexible and attentive to them. When our minds are relaxed, we instinctively think in creative ways, which can help us find our why.

KEY TAKEAWAYS

- Every successful person knows why they do what they do and have strong reasons behind it.
- Until we can find our why, we will continue living our lives on autopilot. We can get thrown off track, lost, and unsure of how to proceed or which way is forward. Even if everything is going well, we might still reflect on the past and wish we had used our time in a different way.
- Finding your why helps give your life meaning, establish a value system, boost your self-esteem, and improve your health.
- Tips on finding your why: knowing what makes you feel alive, figuring out your natural talent, asking for feedback from others, engaging in conversations with new people, turning your suffering into purpose, supporting a cause you care about, and setting aside time for self-care.
- Knowing your why gives you an internal compass that directs all of your choices and takes you on journeys that will enlighten your spirit.

18

BELIEVING IN YOURSELF

*"To be a champ you have to believe in yourself when no one else
will."*- Sugar Ray Robinson

Some believe that success is the result of wealth, luck, or
relationships. While these and various other factors do affect
each person's journey, success depends on our ability to
believe in ourselves. Self-belief is key to self-confidence, which
puts us on the path to success and, together with self-discipline,
helps us stay strong in the face of adversities. When we allow self-
doubts to take over, we become our own worst enemy. By the end
of this chapter, you will learn both how self-belief can benefit you

and how to develop it so that you can become your own biggest supporter in your pursuit of success.

THE ADVANTAGES OF BELIEVING IN YOURSELF

The key to both personal and professional success is self-belief. When you screw up and make a mistake, do you belittle yourself? Do you believe that speaking negatively to yourself will improve you in some way? Making a mistake is one thing, but eventually, we have to accept our mistakes and move forward. Otherwise, we will just be held back by that negative energy. We will not be able to take chances or do what is necessary to get toward our future goals. In the end, we must believe and have confidence in ourselves. We will be one step closer to creating a better life if we do this. Here are some advantages that we can consider in order to believe in ourselves.

YOU ARE THE ONLY ONE WHO CAN DO IT FOR YOURSELF

If we do not think that we will succeed and achieve what we want to do, how on earth would anyone else believe in us? Imagine you want to start a company and have to persuade the investors that your proposal is sound and worth investing in. If you don't truly think that your idea will work, nobody else will have faith in it. As another example, try to picture yourself with no arms or legs. This is the life that Nick Vujicic has to go through (Cama, 2022). At first he doubted his ability to lead a regular life and even tried to commit suicide. However, the turning point came when he started to believe in himself. Now that he is free of these limitations, Nick travels the world and tries to encourage millions of others to have faith in themselves no matter what.

To be sure, having a network of individuals who care about and support us will help a lot, but in the end, only we have the power to seize the opportunities that come our way. We need to have self-belief in order to thrive, and not merely survive in this world.

YOU MOTIVATE YOURSELF TO ACT

Once we can actually picture ourselves crossing the finish line, we become more driven to work toward our goals. We will keep trying until we succeed because we know it is possible and within our grasp. Consider the example of Michael Jordan, one of the most successful NBA players of all time. He has admitted that he had lost hundreds of games and missed thousands of shots before he became famous, but he understood that failure was a necessary part of the process, a source of motivation for him to work even harder and thus the catalyst of his great achievement (Nowik, 2022). We all may benefit from taking a lesson from Michael Jordan's attitude. Just remember that we are only getting closer to success even when we keep failing during our journey.

YOU BANISH NEGATIVE THOUGHTS

We will start seeing positive outcomes once we start thinking positively instead of negatively. How often have you told yourself that you cannot do something? I used to do it far too frequently. Since our minds love to make excuses for things, it is quite simple to come up with an explanation that appears convincing. Positive thoughts and affirmations about ourselves fill our minds, leaving no room for negative ones. And even when these negative ideas occasionally show up, our confident attitude will easily defeat them. For example, if you have an upcoming job interview, you should not get drowned in negative thoughts by thinking that the interviewer will ask hard questions you cannot answer. However, you should prepare different questions which you know the answer to and believe that you will be able to pass the interview because you have prepared yourself for it.

YOU BOOST YOUR CONFIDENCE

If we do not possess enough confidence, the first time we encounter a challenge, we will snap like a twig. Whatever we wish to do in life, there will always be obstacles that cast doubt on our abilities. Holding out hope that we can and will get past them is the only way here. For instance, if you want to launch a new business idea, there will be obstacles that you have to face, such as people's judgments saying that it is a bad idea, the difficulty of finding investors, or even the issue of finding new employees. If you hold on to the belief that you will launch this business, you will be confident that you can solve all of these issues and get through them. This self-confidence comes from a strong internal belief in our own self and capabilities.

YOU MAKE PROGRESS TOWARD SUCCESS AND ACHIEVEMENT

There must be one goal that we have in mind for a while. We are aware of the steps necessary to get there and the successes that have been accomplished by others. Since the pathway is now clear, all that is required of us is the belief that we can succeed before we begin it. By cultivating that optimistic attitude, we will come to understand that the only things standing between us and our goals are time and effort. Our likelihood of achieving our goals significantly rises when we feel like we are getting closer to them.

COMMON CHALLENGES TO SELF-BELIEF

Self-talk that is positive is much easier to say than to do. We must be in charge of our emotions, thoughts, and behavior in order to achieve it. It can be challenging to rewire our brains to think positively instead of negatively. Three common challenges to having self-belief are as follows.

COMPARING YOURSELF TO OTHERS

The key here is perception. Even if we may not be doing great, we might see someone else succeeding. For example, if you have browsed through social media, whether Instagram or TikTok, you must have seen people show off their new sports car or vlog their vacation to a new country. These things may be your dreams as well, and you envy those who have achieved them, but keep in mind that most people share only certain things on social media, and they often are not willing to showcase their difficulties and struggles in life. As the saying goes, "Don't judge a book by its cover." Moreover, there will be time for us to be successful if we try our best and believe in our abilities. We have to stay optimistic and appreciate what we have, without comparing ourselves to others and envying them.

FEARING YOUR PAST

Some say that the past can haunt us, and there is actually some truth to it. Perhaps you had a difficult childhood growing up in a broken family, or you were in an unhealthy relationship with someone who was physically abusive toward you. Although some wounds never heal, you should not let the past define you and hold you back because there is more to you than your trauma. A mental health specialist can help you work through these issues and prevent them from impacting your present.

HAVING TOXIC RELATIONSHIPS

Do you have a partner or friend who constantly criticizes you? Perhaps you fear meeting a parent or a coworker because they often make you feel inferior. Humans are by nature social creatures, but not getting someone's approval can be damaging to your self-esteem. If you feel like you have these kinds of people in your life, it is best that you stay away from them as much as possible. Instead of hanging out with toxic people, seek out new people who can support you so that you will be able to believe in yourself more.

A GUIDE TO BELIEVING IN YOURSELF

Like any critical life skill, self-belief is not developed overnight, but instead requires a lot of time and effort to build through honest reflection, positive thinking, fulfilling relationships, and obviously lots of practice. The challenges we have to face along the way can make it difficult for us to believe in ourselves. In order to help improve our self-belief, here are some guidelines that we can follow.

TAKING COMPLIMENTS GRACEFULLY

It might be hard for people who have extremely low self-esteem to accept compliments. For example, if such a person does not like their appearance and receives compliments about it, they will believe the person complimenting them must be lying in order to be polite. We should focus more on building our confidence if we often respond to praises with sarcasm or by rolling our eyes. However, if we are unable to identify anything nice about ourselves, we can start with the aspects others have praised or complimented us on. We should try to accept the compliment and smile, whether we deem it sincere or not. If we express our gratitude to that person, we will both feel more at ease and happy about it.

HELPING OTHERS

Understanding that we are not struggling with a particular situation that other people are going through helps us appreciate our good fortune, while also motivating us to help those in need. It is deeply satisfying to know that our actions had an impact on someone who needed our assistance. Indeed, although helping others allows us to forget about our problems and shortcomings, it also instantly boosts our self-esteem by bringing our strengths into focus. Thus, the more opportunities we seize to assist, volunteer, mentor, or educate others, the stronger our self-belief becomes as a result.

DOING THINGS THAT YOU FEAR

You are completely mistaken if you think that those who believe in themselves have no fears, anxieties, and second thoughts. For some people, these fears do not become a limitation to their success but rather challenges to improve themselves in the future. The best strategy for conquering fear is to face it head-on instead of running from it, no matter what our fear is—whether public speaking, meeting new people, or negotiating for a raise. Every day, we can try to do something that we fear in order to acquire more power to believe in ourselves from these experiences.

CHANGING YOUR BODY LANGUAGE

Our attitude, body language, and responses to various situations all serve as indicators of how much we believe in ourselves and our levels of self-esteem. Simply modifying our motions and body language can help us to have more self-belief. If others see that we believe in what we do, we will feel more confident in ourselves. Naturally, we can begin with a smile, decent posture, and eye contact with the person we are talking to. Self-belief is reflected in a smile, as well as in high shoulders and a straight back (Belyh, 2019). When we smile, we make others feel more at ease around us, which is a terrific way to enhance our self-belief.

MOVING FORWARD AND NOT LOOKING BACK

In the course of our lives, there will be many situations when we are bound to feel depressed and like giving up. However, we should never listen to the voice in our heads that tells us to quit and causes us to begin doubting ourselves. We must stay strong and keep moving forward until we reach our destination; upon arrival, we will see just how stronger the belief in ourselves and our abilities has grown.

CREATING A LIST OF THINGS YOU ARE PROUD OF

If we are struggling to maintain our self-belief in the face of challenges, we can try making a list of all the things we are most proud of—and thankful for—in our lives, regardless of how trivial they may seem. Furthermore, we need to think of this list as a work-in-progress and constantly update it to reflect our growth mindset. When kept nearby, whether on our work desks or pinned on a wall in our office, the list can serve as a constant reminder of our accomplishments when the going gets too tough.

FEEDING YOUR MIND WITH POSITIVE THINGS

The law of attraction holds some truth to it, in that both the positive and negative energy we put out into the world will eventually come back to us (Perry, 2022). This means that our thinking affects how we engage with the outside world and how others interact with us. How we view ourselves and the world has a lot to do with what we feed our minds with.

For example, we can try to find material that uplifts and inspires us, whether it be through books, films, or social media. Our brains will gradually change their thinking patterns if we frequently read encouraging and inspiring content. We also need to avoid people with negative or cynical viewpoints. Even though it is necessary to be realistic and acknowledge the obstacles life throws in our path, cynicism kills our motivation and undermines our belief in the future, in other people, and ultimately, in ourselves (Perry, 2022).

KEY TAKEAWAYS

- Believing in ourselves is a critical life skill that we need to master. Everyone is special, full of potential, able to grow personally, and deserving of self-belief. If we want to achieve the things we want to do in life, we need to believe in ourselves first because if we won't do it, who will?
- Some benefits that self-belief can offer us: motivating us to act, banishing negative thoughts, boosting our confidence, and enabling our progress toward success and achievement.
- Some challenges to building self-belief: comparing ourselves to others, fearing our past, and having toxic relationships.
- Some strategies for developing self-belief: taking compliments gracefully, helping others in need, doing things that we fear, changing our body language, moving forward and not looking back, creating a list of things we are proud of, and feeding our minds with positive things.
- The power of self-belief lies within each one of us, so it's up to us to let it propel us to success!

CONCLUSION

Now that we have reached the end of the book, I hope that you enjoyed learning some helpful tips for developing consistent self-discipline and that you will put them to good use. Remember, though, that all the insights and strategies that were covered here are just the first step on your journey toward self-discipline, and the next step is taking action. No matter how many books you read, nothing will actually change unless you actively implement the great ideas they teach you.

That being said, you may find that only some of the suggestions and exercises for training your mental muscle presented in this book apply, or maybe appeal, to you. In other words, you should not expect to immediately start making changes in every area of your life. You can choose one or two skills you would like to strengthen, or areas in which you need to improve, then move on from there once you are pleased with the outcome. Not only will you have developed stronger self-discipline in the process, but the fresh energy that such discipline provides will also prime you for the next challenge.

For example, if you are concerned about your physical health and fitness, then this is what you should focus on: establishing better and healthier habits. After all, if your body is not healthy, you will not be able to accomplish anything else in life. In order to make this vital change, you will need to exercise self-discipline.

Now, the key to developing mental toughness and self-discipline is commitment to your goals and consistency in pursuing them no matter the challenges at hand. By staying the course and sticking to your habit in order to successfully meet long-term goals in one area of life, such as health and fitness, it will be easier to accomplish similar goals in other areas. As it is often said, success breeds success, so it's important that you first achieve a small measure of success before aiming higher.

In addition to defining self-discipline and explaining its benefits, this book details the steps to take, the skills to practice, and strategies to adopt in order to become more self-disciplined. These ideas are highlighted at the end of each chapter that invites you to set specific goals and discover your why, try to do something that sucks, let go of things that you cannot change, take responsibility for your life, practice delayed gratification, stop listening to the naysayers, find a mentor to guide you, as well as an accountability partner, visualize your success, and last, but not least, believe in yourself!

If you possess the drive to succeed but are unsure where to start, I hope you will pick up this book and find guidance and inspiration in it. And if you have already set out on your journey to success, but there comes a time when you feel lost or disheartened, use this book as a stepping stone to help you find your way and regain confidence in yourself and your abilities to turn your vision of success into reality.

Everything worthwhile in life takes effort and time. Only those who can demonstrate discipline, determination, and dedication will reap the benefits of reaching their goals.

REFERENCES

Abdou, A. (2022, October 20). *7 key differences between having a growth mindset versus a fixed mindset.* The Ladders. https://www.theladders.com/career-advice/7-key-differences-between-having-a-growth-mindset-versus-a-fixed-mindset

Ali, A. (2021, February 9). *5 ways to be more self-disciplined and achieve your goals.* LinkedIn. https://www.linkedin.com/pulse/5-ways-more-self-disciplined-achieve-your-goals-dr-adnan-ali/

Arrington, C. (2022, February 1). *7 keys to successfully mastering self-discipline.* Candy Arrington. https://candyarrington.com/7-keys-to-successfully-mastering-self-discipline/

Bastos, F. (2019, January 3). *Control what you can: how to focus your energy in the right places.* Mind Owl. https://mindowl.org/control-what-you-can-control/

Belyh, A. (2019, November 25). *The incredible power of believing in yourself.* Cleverism. https://www.cleverism.com/the-incredible-power-of-believing-in-yourself/

Benefits of an accountability partner in business. (2022). Christian Women's Corner. https://www.christianwomenscorner.com/accountability-partner.html

Bokhari, D. (2022). *The ultimate guide to developing self-discipline.* Dean Bokhari. https://www.deanbokhari.com/the-guide-to-developing-self-discipline/

Bradi, K. (2022). *7 ways to eliminate your excuses.* Lifehack. https://www.lifehack.org/articles/productivity/7-ways-eliminate-your-excuses.html

Braun, K. (2023, January 9). *How an accountability partner can help you succeed.* Clever Girl Finance. https://www.clevergirlfinance.com/blog/accountability-partner/

Cama, M. (2022, October 26). *A life without limbs: Nick Vujicic uses his story to inspire students across globe.* Eagle Nation Online. https://eaglenationonline.com/44285/features/a-life-without-limbs-nick-vujicic-uses-his-story-to-inspire-students-across-the-globe/

Canelas, F. (2021, July 11). *7 reasons why you should (really) plan your days.* (2021, July 11). Filipa Canelas. https://www.filipacanelas.com/blog/7-reasons-why-https://www.lifehack.org/articou-should-plan-your-days

Casano, T. (2022, March 16). *10 ways to believe in yourself again.* Lifehack. https://www.lifehack.org/288536/10-ways-believe-yourself-again

Castrillon, C. (2020, march, 8). *How suzy batiz bootstrapped her way to a $240 million empire.* Forbes. https://www.forbes.com/sites/carolinecastrillon/2020/03/08/how-suzy-batiz-bootstrapped-her-way-to-a-240-million-empire/?sh=77eb9f785fea

Celes. (2022). *7 important reasons why you should set goals.* Personal Excellence. https://personalexcellence.co/blog/why-set-goals/

Clear, J. (2018). *Atomic habit summary.* James Clear. https://jamesclear.com/atomic-habits-summary

Clear, J. (2020). *Atomic habits – book summary notes/highlights.* Ali Abdaal. https://aliabdaal.com/book-notes/atomic-habits-summary/

Clear, J. (2022). *How to build a new habit: this is your strategy guide.* James Clear. https://jamesclear.com/habit-guide

Clements, R. (2022). *10 ways to ignore the naysayers and achieve your dreams.* Lifehack. https://www.lifehack.org/articles/productivity/10-ways-ignore-the-naysayers-and-achieve-your-dreams.html

Consequences of lack of discipline. (2020, July 15). The Ellegee. https://www.theellegee.com/blog/consequencese-of-lack-of-discipline

D'Angelo, M. (2022, August 6). *How to find a mentor.* Business News Daily. https://www.businessnewsdaily.com/6248-how-to-find-mentor.html

Davy, P. (2019, November 3). *Do something that sucks, every day.* Medium. https://medium.com/@paul_37208/do-something-that-sucks-every-day-abcfbdd43df2

Demers, J. (2022). *7 ways successful people spend their free time.* Inc. https://www.inc.com/jayson-demers/7-ways-successful-people-spend-their-free-time.html

Downey, L. (2022, June 19). *Mark Zuckerberg: Founder and CEO of Meta (formerly Facebook).* Investopedia. https://www.investopedia.com/terms/m/mark-zuckerberg.asp

Finkelstein, D. (2020, June 30). *Why should you have an accountability partner.* LinkedIn. https://www.linkedin.com/pulse/why-should-you-have-accountability-partner-darren-finkelstein/

Finkelstein, D. (2022). *What are the benefits of an accountability partner?* Tick Those Boxes. https://tickthoseboxes.com.au/what-are-the-benefits-of-an-accountability-partner/#:~:text=They%20Provide%20Support%20And%20Advice,require%20more%20attention%20and%20focus.

Firsich, M. (2020, May 22). *Do something that sucks today.* LinkedIn. https://www.linkedin.com/pulse/do-something-sucks-today-michael-firsich/

5 easy ways to gain the self-discipline to reach your goals. (2017, October 25). Absolute Cycle Bangkok. http://absolutecyclebangkok.com/5-easy-ways-to-gain-self-discipline-to-reach-your-goals/

5 reasons to ignore naysayers and pave your own pathway to success. (2018, January 19). Forbes. https://www.forbes.com/sites/steveolenski/2018/01/19/5-reasons-to-ignore-naysayers-and-pave-your-own-pathway-to-success/?sh=7919f5681e87

5 things successful people do that others don't. (2016, May 24). American Express. https://www.americanexpress.com/en-us/business/trends-and-insights/articles/5-things-successful-people-do-that-others-dont/

Goeke, N. (2018, November 29). *Atomic habits summary.* Four Minute Books. https://fourminutebooks.com/atomic-habits-summary/#:~:text=1%2DSentence%2DSummary%3A%20Atomic,massive%2C%20positive%20change%20over%20time.

Griggs, U. (2022, May 30). *How to stop making excuses and start taking responsibility.* Lifehack. https://www.lifehack.org/articles/mentalstrength/how-to-stop-making-excuses-and-get-what-you-want.html

Herrity, J. (2022, July 2). *How do you set SMART goals? Definition and examples.* Indeed. https://www.indeed.com/career-advice/career-development/smart-goals

How to build healthy habits in your daily life. (2022). Parodontax. https://www.parodontax.com/amp/how-to-build-healthy-habits.html

How to focus on what you can control (and win more battles). (2021, November 16). Soulsalt. https://soulsalt.com/focus-on-what-you-can-control/

How to plan your day: Benefits and 8 tips for success. (2021, November 25). Indeed. https://www.indeed.com/career-advice/career-development/how-to-plan-your-day

How to take responsibility for your life. (2022). Live About. https://www.liveabout.com/how-to-take-responsibility-for-your-life-1919214

Imafidon, C. (2022). *15 small things successful people do every day.* Lifehack.

https://www.lifehack.org/articles/productivity/15-small-things-successful-people-every-day.html

Ivers, I. (2020, July 22). *7 practical ways to stop making excuses.* Ivy Ivers. https://ivyivers.com/feel-good/7-practical-tips-to-stop-making-excuses/

Khan, H. (2021, February 27). *Discipline will take you to places where motivation can`t.* linkedIn. https://www.linkedin.com/pulse/discipline-take-you-places-where-motivation-cant-hamza-khan/

Khurana, R. (2021, August 13). *Ignore the naysayers from your life.* LinkedIn. https://www.linkedin.com/pulse/ignore-naysayers-from-your-life-rupinder-khurana/

Krbechek, A & Tagle, A. (2022). *Motivation is an unreliable emotion.* Npr. https://www.npr.org/2019/10/25/773158390/how-to-find-a-mentor-and-make-it-work

Lack of self-discipline. (2021, December 10). Evolve Inc. https://evolveinc.io/self-improvement/self-discipline/lack-of-self-discipline/

Manson, M. (2022). *The responsibility/fault fallacy.* Mark Manson. https://markmanson.net/responsibility-fault-fallacy

McNaney, J. (2015, February 12). *5 benefits we can reap from the power of visualization immediately.* Huff Post. https://www.huffpost.com/entry/5-benefits-we-can-reap-fr_b_6672638

Moe, K. (2021, June 4). *5 visualization techniques to help you reach your goals.* Better Up. https://www.betterup.com/blog/visualization

184

Morin, A. (2022, December 26). *Tips for finding your purpose in life*. Very Well Mind. https://www.verywellmind.com/tips-for-finding-your-purpose-in-life-4164689

Murphy, A. (2021, April 22). *9 ways to take responsibility for your life*. Declutter the Mind. https://declutterthemind.com/blog/take-responsibility/

Navided, A. (2020, November 27). *Marshmallow test experiment and delayed gratification*. Simply Psychology. https://www.simplypsychology.org/marshmallow-test.html

Ngako, P. (2022, March 12). *10 tips for using visualization for success*. LinkedIn. https://www.linkedin.com/pulse/10-tips-using-visualization-success-patrick-ngako-cpa-1c/?trk=articles_directory

Nowik, O. (2022). *7 powerful reasons why you should believe in yourself*. Lifehack. https://www.lifehack.org/articles/communication/7-powerful-reasons-why-you-should-believe-yourself.html

Parincu, Z. (2022). *Self-discipline: Definition, tips, & how to develop it*. Berkeley Wellbeing Institute. https://www.berkeleywellbeing.com/self-discipline.html

Pate, D. (2019, April 1). *7 myths about discipline you need to stop believing*. Entrepreneur. https://www.entrepreneur.com/living/7-myths-about-discipline-you-need-to-stop-believing/331400

Patel, N. (2022). *How to find a mentor online*. Neil Patel. https://neilpatel.com/blog/find-mentor/

Perry, E. (2022). *How to walk the freeing path of believing in yourself.* Better Up. https://www.betterup.com/blog/how-to-believe-yourself

Phelps. B. (2022). *The importance of keeping promises to yourself: Part 1.* Upside Therapy. https://www.upsidertherapy.com/blog/the-importance-of-keeping-promises-to-yourself#:~:text=Each%20time%20we%20keep%20a,follo w%20through%20on%20our%20commitments

Robbins, T. (2022). *Importance of delayed gratification.* Tony Robbins. https://www.tonyrobbins.com/achieve-lasting-weight-loss/delayed-gratification/

Robinson, J. *Motivation or discipline?* (2022, August 8). Nasdaq. https://www.nasdaq.com/articles/motivation-or-discipline

Roepe, L. (2022). *10 tips for finding a mentor-and making the relationship count.* themuse. https://www.themuse.com/advice/how-to-find-a-mentor

Sasson, R. (2022). What is self-discipline? Definitions and Meaning. Success Consciousness. https://www.successconsciousness.com/blog/inner-strength/what-is-self-discipline/

Satterfield, D. (2020, February 14). *Discipline comes from within you.* The Leader Maker. https://www.theleadermaker.com/discipline-comes-from-within-you/

Scherr, M. (2022, July 21). *Successful people do the things that unsuccessful people won't.* linkedIn. https://www.linkedin.com/pulse/successful-people-do-things-unsuccessful-wont-michele-cole-scherr-/?trk=pulse-article_more-articles_related-content-card

Self-discipline for students. (2022). UO People. https://www.uopeople.edu/blog/self-discipline-for-students/

Self-discipline. (2022). Mind Tools. https://www.mindtools.com/adjf7nz/self-discipline

Stop living on autopilot. (2022). Hack Spirit. https://hackspirit.com/taking-responsibility/

Successful people do what unsuccessful people are not willing to do. (2022). Quotespedia. https://www.quotespedia.org/authors/j/jim-rohn/successful-people-do-what-unsuccessful-people-are-not-willing-to-do-dont-wish-it-were-easier-wish-you-were-better-jim-rohn/

Susman, D. (2022, February 17). *How to face your fears.* Very Well Mind. https://www.verywellmind.com/healthy-ways-to-face-y our-fears-4165487

Taking in the risk in life: 5 steps for determining worthwhile risks and achieving your goals. (2022, April 27). Soul Salt. https://soulsalt.com/taking-a-risk-in-life/#:~:text=Taking%20risks%20can%20change%20you,and%20can%20do%20it%20again.

10 things successful people do every day. (2022). Keep Inspiring. https://www.keepinspiring.me/10-things-successful-people-do-every-day/

Thakur, V. (2019, September 16). *Top 10 benefits of discipline.* LinkedIn. https://www.linkedin.com/pulse/top-10-benefits-discipline-vipan-thakur/
187

The benefits of planning your day the night before instead of in the morning. (2022). Amazing Marvin. https://blog.amazingmarvin.com/6-benefits-of-planning-your-day-the-night-before-instead-of-in-the-morning/

The power of taking full responsibility for your life. (2022, March 22). Gregg Van Ourek. https://greggvanourek.com/full-responsibility/

The powerful ways to cultivate extreme self-discipline. (2022). Forbes. https://www.forbes.com/sites/brentgleeson/2020/08/25/8-powerful-ways-to-cultivate-extreme-self-discipline/?sh=74090db6182d

The reasons why mentorship is important for mentee and mentor. (2022, August 30). https://www.indeed.com/career-advice/career-development/why-is-a-mentor-important

Tony, T. (2022). *How to stop making excuses.* Tony Robbins. https://www.tonyrobbins.com/productivity-performance/how-to-stop-making-excuses/

Turner, C. (2016, July 27). *Is discipline a choice?* Meetatroam. https://meetatroam.com/2016/07/is-discipline-a-choice/

Understanding laser focus, how to develop it and boost your productivity. (2022). Student Lesson. https://studentlesson.com/what-is-laser-focus-and-how-can-you-develop-it/

Ward, M. (2016, November 16). *Warren Buffett's reading routine could make you smarter, science suggests.* CNBC. https://www.cnbc.com/2016/11/16/warren-buffettsreading-routine-could-make-you-smarter-suggests-science.html

Warrel, M. (2013m October 30). Do you know your why? 4 questions to tap the power of purpose. Forbes. https://www.forbes.com/sites/margiewarrell/2013/10/30/know-your-why-4-questions-to-tap-the-power-of-purpose/?sh=380fb87473ad

Waters, S. (2021, June, 23). *How delayed gratification changes the way you live and work.* Better Up. https://www.betterup.com/blog/delayed-gratification#:~:text=Delayed%20gratification%20is%20the%20ability,for%20what%20you%20truly%20want.

What are atomic habits, and why use them to create your L&D strategy. (2022). Iseazy. https://www.iseazy.com/blog/atomic-habits/#:~:text=Atomic%20habits%20are%20small%2C%20repetitive,changes%20in%20our%20everyday%20lives.

Willis, A. (2022). *5 benefits of finding your purpose.* They Call Me Blessed. https://www.theycallmeblessed.org/5-benefits-finding-your-purpose/

Wooll, M. (2021, October 19). *Start finding your purpose and unlock your best life.* Better Up. https://www.betterup.com/blog/finding-purpose

Write down five positive things from each day. (2022). No Panic. https://nopanic.org.uk/write-down-five-positive-things-from-each-day/

Yeti, S. (2021, August 4). *Consequences you would face if you lack self-discipline.* Success Yeti.

https://www.successyeti.com/happiness/consequences-you-would-face-if-you-lack-self-discipline/2021/08/04

Yetman, D. (2021, June 21). *Exposure therapy*. Healthline. https://www.healthline.com/health/exposure-therapy#definition

Zimmerman, B. J. & Kitsantas, A. (2014). Comparing students' self-discipline and self-regulation measures and their prediction of academic achievement. *Contemporary Education Psychology, 39*(2), 145–155.

THE POWER OF MENTAL TOUGHNESS

DISCOVER HOW TO BUILD MENTAL TOUGHNESS AND CONTROL YOUR THOUGHTS IN ORDER TO ACHIEVE AT THE HIGHEST LEVELS

WILLIAM ANDERSON

INTRODUCTION

To succeed, you need mental toughness: the confidence and resilience of an individual that indicates how influential he or she may be at work, in personal relationships, and in education. In addition, you need grit, which describes someone who has a strong sense of character.

How often have you pictured a life that is more substantial than the one you are living? There is something holding you back from reaching your potential and making choices that impact your life in a positive way. It's easy to feel that life is unfair and there is little you can do to change it—that you are stuck in a loop of one step forward and then one enormous landslide backward.

I grew up in Romania, an ex-communist country. The revolution took place in 1989 and I was born in 1996 into a country that was already poor. My parents could afford very little while caring for six children on my father's salary. I always dreamed big and wanted to dedicate my life to something meaningful. I wanted to play professional soccer in Europe, but since we didn't have the money to send me to a city where I could join a team to fulfill my goal, I was forced to let this dream go.

Schoolwork wasn't my strength since I found it difficult to focus—I later discovered that I had ADHD. At age 18, I saw a fitness influencer, Jeff Seid, who was so motivated and dedicated to his elite fitness. I was inspired to become a fitness influencer as well. I said goodbye to Romania and moved to several countries throughout Europe to chase my dream, all while working up to 12 hours a day. At the same time, I was working out early in the morning, and waking up at 3 AM. I made all of these sacrifices to obtain the PRO CARD in the Men's Physique Division.

After several injuries and my body giving up on me despite my drive, I went back to Romania and, with much hard work, began a business that eventually made a profit. This success, through all my failings and getting back up, made me realize that my true path led me to write this book to encourage others to never give up on making something meaningful of their goals, of their lives.

The difficulty doesn't always lie in knowing what you want to get out of life, but in knowing how to achieve the goals and standards that you have set out for yourself. Dreams and goals are not achieved by putting them out into the universe or wishing on a double rainbow. They are achieved by becoming mentally prepared for hard work and by using the power of mental toughness to build your life to the highest level of success.

The secret to success? It's all in your mind.

Your ability to do great things lies in your ability to convince yourself that you can achieve greatness. Mental strength is a concept that relates directly to traits associated with and interchangeable with persistence, strength, resilience (Cleveland Clinic, 2022), emotional regulation, and a positive outlook. All of these qualities will help establish how likely you are to visualize and bring to fruition your dreams.

Through this book, I will guide you toward realizing your inner strength and how to increase your mental toughness so that you can reach your goals through hard work, planning, and self-realization. Mental toughness can be improved through

- establishing pertinent goals.

- abiding by your body's needs.

- focusing on meaningful tasks and projects.

- acknowledging and healing feelings of negativity.

- pushing beyond your comfort zone.

Mental toughness is key to achieving your goals in life, including work, home life, and health goals. You will learn that there is more to setting up and establishing your goals than planning, but hard work and the ability to repel negative energy from others will help set the stage for how your life plays out.

You will learn what mental toughness is, where it comes from, and why it is crucial for your success. You will learn that mental strength has no poster child and that anyone is capable, not only those who appear rugged, and why today's generation and accessibility to social media is breeding self-pity and a lazier outlook on what it takes to earn your worth.

Everyone is traveling a different journey through this life; where we end up is determined by the effort we put in and the risks we take as we go along. There are battles that you will face and times that you will want to give up, so you will learn how to use the storms to reap lusher rewards and use the broken pieces of shattered dreams and the chants of naysayers to build a life from the mosaic of broken glass.

Many components of life take mental toughness and everyone is capable of hard work. Whether you are building your dream business, working through university, joining the military, or saving up to buy your first home, you will get there through determination and grit.

Acknowledge that your journey will be challenging and then set out knowing that you will have to break down walls, including your own, to make things happen. Associate with like-minded people who are building their own mental strength and who accept that their failures can be overcome through their own determination.

While you read through this journey to mental toughness, use a pencil to make notes or highlight key components that you want to revisit later. If you like to keep your books free of markings, use sticky notes or fold the corners of the pages to find notable points later on. If you have the ebook, grab a pad of paper and make key notes as you go along.

The power of mental toughness is a journey that begins now.

WHAT IS MENTAL TOUGHNESS AND WHERE DOES IT COME FROM

Mental toughness refers to someone who is comfortable with who they are and can take the challenges that life throws at them with ease. Mental toughness isn't to be confused with arrogance or narcissism, but rather the confidence that one has in their ability to succeed, even when things seem insurmountable.

Building mental toughness or mental strength is essential to living your life to the fullest. Developing your mental health, using a variety of tools and various techniques will allow you to push for what you truly want and not let obstacles scare you off of your chosen path.

In addition to building meaningful connections with others and building self-esteem, strong mental strength gives us the courage to try things that frighten us and allows us to cope with challenging events and situations that occur in life.

Mental health is largely similar to mental strength but they are, in fact, different.

You know what mental strength is but you may not know that mental health is defined as one's emotional well-being. However, even if you do not suffer from depression, anxiety, or another form of mental illness, you may not have mental toughness. In fact, you may have anxiety and struggle with depression but be a mentally strong individual. To break it down:

Mental health is

- having a mental health issue or the absence of a mental health issue.

- your state of mental well-being overall.

Mental strength is

- having a grip on and understanding of your emotions.

- being able to handle negative situations in a positive way.

- knowing when to indulge your emotions and the ability to set them aside.

The idea behind mental toughness is to be strong when faced with adversity, but this is not something that we all can do. Mental strength takes consistent work, challenging yourself, and not letting anyone else get into your head.

Emotional regulation is key to mental toughness because it allows us to exercise control over our emotions. To have emotional regulation is to have the ability to challenge the situation we are in and rethink the outcome and what we can do to get there. It requires us to control our anger, anxiety, and fear, and refocus our thoughts in a more productive manner.

HOW TO BUILD YOUR MENTAL TOUGHNESS

Everyone, with determination, is capable of gaining mental toughness. Just as consistent exercises are necessary to help shape and strengthen your muscles to withstand injury, mental toughness can be built through a series of mental exercises.

COGNITIVE EXERCISES

These allow you to change your way of thinking by way of establishing a mindset that helps you maintain a positive outlook and rework any negative thoughts or reinvent a realistic mindset from one of self-doubt. Some ways to establish and practice cognitive exercises may include (Cleveland Clinic, 2022):

- Keeping a gratitude diary that acknowledges what you have and affirms feelings of positivity and thoughts of gratitude.

- Argue for the opposition when you find yourself dwelling on all that could go wrong. Instead, consider all that could go exactly as you have planned for it to go.

- Empathize with yourself and offer compassion to yourself when mistakes are made, as you would a friend. We are often much harder on ourselves than we would be on anyone that we consider a loved one.

EMOTIONAL EXERCISES

These exercises help heighten your awareness of your emotional position and give you the ability to see it as useful. These may help you to manage uncomfortable feelings or reduce the magnitude of negative emotions or those that cause ill effects. These exercises can be:

- Labeling how you feel so that you can take a step back and see them from a different perspective. This may allow you to see your emotions for what they are and help alleviate the darkness they have over you. Rather than focusing on negative feelings, change your mindset by going for a walk in the fresh air or allow yourself to say the feeling out loud but then reaffirm that you are not what those feelings imply.

BEHAVIORAL EXERCISES

These include doing what will help you feel your best and allow you to live your best and happiest life. There are some behavioral exercises you can do.

Schedule positive activities to do for yourself, with or without someone else. This can be anything from having a spa day to reading a book or going paddleboarding. Anything that reaffirms that you are alive and doing well while also giving you some much-needed self-reflection, is going to help you realize that you are worth your accomplishments.

There are three essential components to building your mental toughness:

1. Realistic Thinking

    Realistic thinking is critical to mental toughness because it demonstrates the ability to recognize irrational thoughts and reimagine them as more pragmatic concepts. This reasoning allows you to recognize when you are being critical of your efforts or emotions and rework your inner voice to be more compassionate.

2. Acknowledging Your Feelings

    Having mental strength is not about being above pain or holding back emotions, but rather acknowledging how you are feeling and understanding why. The ability to take a deep breath and accept that you are feeling unpleasant is a sign of mental toughness.

3. Taking Positive Action

    A great sign of mental toughness is taking productive steps toward affirmative action in your goals or even with self-care. This refers to anything that moves you toward making your life more positive.

WAYS TO BUILD MENTAL STRENGTH

Mental toughness is a key component to the success of elite athletes, entrepreneurs, doctors, nurses, paramedics, firemen, police officers, writers, teachers, parents, and so on. To become successful in any one of these professions or in raising a family, you need to have grit, determination, and a will to overcome all odds.

Striving to achieve mental toughness and persevere is a notable goal and the concept is understandable, but what does mental strength look like every day?

Elite athletes that are mentally strong are consistent and resilient. They hit their workouts without fail, push themselves past their limits, and always support those around them.

Community and business leaders strive to get the job done, be consistent, and set clear and attainable goals that they strive for every day. Negative comments and challenging times do not prevent them from moving forward toward their goals and they encourage others to stay the course along their own paths to success. These leaders build others up because they understand there is strength in supporting others.

Editors, writers, and other artists are consistent in the schedules they keep and the deadlines they face. They are committed to doing a good job and set out to do a good job in the time they have allotted. I would not have been able to write this book without the inspiration to put together a concise plan and the determination to follow through.

Having perseverance and determination doesn't need to be something you took to from the time you were a child; it can be earned by developing mental toughness. Some strategies that are effective in building mental toughness in life include:

DEFINING WHAT MENTAL TOUGHNESS MEANS TO YOU

Everyone has their own definition of what it means to be mentally tough. To an athlete, it might be rebuilding after an injury, but to you it might mean

- eating a clean diet for a month to help lose weight.

- adding a repetition to your workout every week to build up muscle mass.

- taking a night class to help you change careers.

- beating a work deadline rather than aiming to get it done right on time.

Set a clear idea about the goal you set for yourself. While being mentally strong is abstract and different for everyone, it is how we build a stronger connection to tangible actions.

BUILDING MENTAL TOUGHNESS

Applying mental strength to exceptional circumstances isn't the only way to build strength. It isn't only about coming back from a devastating loss or buying your first house after you lose everything. These extreme circumstances absolutely build perseverance and strengthen resolve, but they are not the only thing that builds mental strength.

Small, everyday challenges and wins help build mental toughness, as working out every day and gradually building your muscles are going to build a stronger base than running a triathlon every three months without preparation.

Showing yourself that you can do one more pull-up, walk one more mile, and put in an extra hour a day to finish a house project will help build up confidence in yourself and prove that you are capable every day—not only when all the chips are down.

FINDING THE ROOTS OF MENTAL TOUGHNESS

Mental toughness comes from habits, not impulses. Being strong, mentally, isn't about pulling on a cape and entering superhero mode on the odd occasion it is necessary; it's about consistently sticking to your schedule or steamrolling challenges time and again. Those who are mentally tough do not need an abundance of courage or necessarily have the brains to attend Yale University— they need habits that build a foundation of reliance.

You can build mental strength through cognitive, emotional, and behavioral exercises. Building mental strength will help you become less likely to adapt to the expectation of others and fall into negative comments. Mental toughness will help you make thought-out, intentional decisions that will benefit you on your path to a better life.

CHALLENGE YOURSELF: INCREASE TOUGH THINKING

A strong mind is needed for mental toughness. A strong mind allows you to control your thoughts, have positive self-talk, and stay in a mindset that makes thriving much easier. To maintain this positive mindset, you need to acknowledge when you are caught in a negative thought pattern so you can use learned techniques to redirect your thinking to positive action.

The ability to recognize negative thinking will allow you to reset to positive thoughts and manage your emotions. When you identify negativity creeping in, you can establish boundaries within yourself to help you turn it into useful thinking.

The exercise that you need to practice is called thought-stopping. This is the action of suppressing undesirable thoughts and acts as a way to disrupt a pattern of negative thinking and direct your efforts and thoughts into something that helps alleviate stress and not induce it, with the goal of preventing unhelpful behaviors from triggering you in the first place.

The first step is to acknowledge when your thoughts are turning negative. The second step allows you to choose from one of three options:

1. Instantly imagine a flashing red light.

2. Instantly tell yourself to stop.

3. Instantly do both.

These simple steps will defer the negative thought and reset your way of thinking to a more constructive solution.

KEY TAKEAWAYS

In this chapter, you learned that:

- building mental toughness or mental strength is essential to living your life to the fullest.

- there are three essential components to building your mental toughness–realistic thinking, acknowledging your feelings, and taking positive action.

- mental strength can be built through cognitive, emotional, and behavioral exercises. Building mental strength will help you become less likely to adapt to the expectation of others and fall into negative comments.

2

WHY BEING MENTALLY TOUGH IS SO IMPORTANT

We are all born with the potential to be mentally tough, but it takes perseverance and a sense of urgency. Being mentally tough is a mindset that can be taught and learned by anyone. People who have earned mental strength have attributes that lead to them being more successful, such as being more determined, showing consistency, and reaping better results in their job, personal life, and goals. Other benefits include (Yeong, 2017):

1. Feeling of contentment

    When you have mental toughness you are more likely to feel content in life, have less stress, not struggle with mental health illness, and to rest better at night. Those who are mentally tough are less likely to let others get away with bullying them because they know their worth.

2. Aspiration and perseverance

When you are mentally tough, you are able to handle more stress, which means you push yourself beyond your comfort zone. It will help you overcome a lack of purpose and urge you to keep going when your mind is trying to convince you to surrender your ambition.

3. Positive outlook

Those who possess mental strength have a more positive attitude and a more hopeful outlook on how well things can turn out. They are also more likely to try new activities and extend their abilities to volunteering and helping to provide a more positive environment for others.

4. Greater performance

With mental strength comes the confidence to deliver on expectations of oneself, which extends to social commitments and relationships, as well as producing more output in these areas.

When you are mentally strong, you will be more confident in your work, have firm boundaries in relationships, and be more reliable in general because mentally tough people do not pull out of obligations.

5. Greater self-worth

No one is immune to feeling inadequate or questioning their ability from time to time, but it is mental strength that keeps those feelings from overtaking your potential. When your own mind is challenging your ability, it's not always easy to overcome, but when you are prepared, you are able to ignore the negativity that swirls in your head and persevere.

6. Use failures as strength

    Any failure can be saddled with feelings of awkwardness or embarrassment which can deter many from carrying on with their goals. With mental strength comes the ability to take failure and transform the negative into stepping stones to avoid entering into the patterns or decisions that lead to the same mistakes. Failure breeds learning opportunities and should be collected and moved on.

7. Helps refute negativity

    There are those who believe they know everything, even what's best for you. Mental toughness helps reject bad advice that others may offer. Feeling confident in your self-worth will help take negative criticism and set it aside rather than carry it alongside you. You will feel confident enough to move on without debating the issues someone may have.

DAILY HABITS THAT WILL IMPROVE MENTAL STRENGTH

Mental strength, as mentioned, is not something you are born with or will come into naturally by going through adversity. Just as you need to exercise to build your physical strength, building mental strength happens over time with consistency and habit-building.

Some habits that will help you build your mental toughness include:

1. Express thanks: Remind yourself to be thankful every day for what you have, without focusing on the negative. By acknowledging the things you are grateful for—whether by writing it in a journal, saying it as a daily affirmation, or thinking to yourself—you are pushing out any negative thoughts that can bog down the mind.

2. Shut out all distractions: Take fifteen minutes each day to sit and be with your own thoughts. Sitting in the silence of your own space and shutting out all distractions is essential to building mental toughness.

3. Push beyond your comfort zone: Take the time every day to push yourself beyond what is easy or comfortable. Going to

the gym even though you feel tired, asking for an assignment at work that you really want, or asserting yourself at the forefront of a conversation will all help to build your confidence and help prove to yourself that you are willing to do what once seemed out of reach.

4. Take responsibility for yourself: Blaming others for your unfortunate circumstances is going to keep you stuck in a place of self-pity. Rather than using language such as, "my friends make me feel inadequate," choose to rephrase it as, "I am the one who controls how I feel."

5. Treat yourself with kindness: Instigating a kind and supportive inner voice creates a sense of self-compassion. Speak to yourself as you would if you were speaking to a friend and be encouraging rather than critical. Your inner voice should also be strong enough to put you in check if you are sliding into self-loathing or avoiding accountability for your actions.

6. Acknowledge and identify your feelings: It should be a daily habit to address your feelings–good and bad–to determine how they may be affecting the choices you make. Making choices that will have a negative impact can occur when we allow our feelings to run rampant without considering how the highest highs or the lowest lows may affect our decision.

7. Utilize your mental energy productively: Wasting time on things that occurred in the past or worrying about an outcome that you have no control over will take an emotional toll and waste your time. Save your mental energy for things that you can solve and for reframing the negative into a positive solution or next step.

You now know that mental toughness is the ability to perform optimally on a consistent basis in any situation that you find yourself in. You don't have to be at the top level of your sport, business, or whatever else you are climbing toward to have mental toughness.

Mental toughness is what will get you ahead in any aspect of your life that you strive to do better in. Building habits that strengthen your mental toughness is key to fulfilling your goals. Below are some exercises that can help you improve your mental toughness.

EXERCISES THAT WILL HELP IMPROVE YOUR MENTAL TOUGHNESS

Just as an elite athlete needs to consistently practice to build their muscle memory in their sport of choice, mental toughness can only be strengthened through consistent work and dedication to making decisions that will lead to your goals.

There are daily exercises that can be done to improve your mental toughness. With practice, these techniques will help you overcome mental weakness without even thinking about it.

Visualize the outcome you want: Those with uncertain thoughts know what it's like to wake up and go to bed with the same lingering thoughts—Did I perform well enough for the promotion? Will I get the job or did I blow the interview? Am I raising happy children?

Take those negative and nagging thoughts and turn them into optimistic phrases that encourage a more positive outcome—the best scenario there could be. You may think that this is a sure way to build up hope only to be met with disappointment if things don't work out, but it's not the case. Building a positive expectation will help you build the mental expectation that you are capable and deserving of good things. Envisioning a positive outcome will create more chances of greatness than negativity.

Make anxiety work for you: Malleability is what allows our brains to be resilient when we go through difficulties. It is the reason we are able to take a breath, assess the situation, and rethink our decisions and thoughts to make more calculated decisions. Remind yourself that anxiety is not necessarily a detriment.

- Anger can hinder our performance and progress or it can sharpen our aim, improve our accessibility to motivating thoughts, and give clarity to what should come first.

- Sadness can deflate our motivation or it can reignite motivation that will lead to changes and strength in our behavior and help us change our circumstances or environment.

- Worrying about failure can lead to avoidance of effort to accomplish your goals or it can help you set more distinguished steps to move you along your path with more achievable goals and help you narrow your motivation.

- Fear is a powerful deterrent when you allow it to remind you of what you failed to accomplish or you can use it to learn from your mistakes and redirect yourself to other opportunities.

- Disappointment can rob you of motivation or light a fire that will challenge you to do better or try to do more.

When broken down, these may seem like simple examples, but engaging in these practices will help lead you to concrete choices that create concrete outcomes.

Get outdoors: Research has proven that getting back to nature has powerful effects on improving the quality of our mental health and resilience. Spending time on mountain trails, on the water, or going for a walk in the park will all lift your spirits and create a bond with nature which increases serotonin levels and helps restore energy and balance your equilibrium.

Recognize your support network: Building mental toughness is reliant on having a support network of family and friends that will be there to help support you through challenging times. Knowing that someone is there when you need them will lessen anxiety.

When you are feeling distressed, it is easy to hide inside yourself and withdraw from those around you, social activities, and your goals. When you know you have someone backing you, it offers confidence and a push to carry on, even in the most trying times.

Habitual practices and daily exercises will help you build your mental toughness. By using visualization techniques and simple meditation or getting outdoors, you can clear your mind of the negative, making room for productive thoughts.

If someone talks about a goal they want to accomplish but then follows up with, "But I don't have time," that is weakness talking. If you have something important to you, you will make the time; that is mental strength.

There is a hospice in Vancouver, Canada, called Canuck Place Children's Hospice. It is the first hospice for children ever in North America and offers respite to parents and a place for families to stay when they visit doctors in the Vancouver area but live far away. The parents know their children will never grow up. Knowing that they have a terminally ill child, no doubt, devastated them, but they did not give up on giving that child the best life they could in the time that they have left. The mental toughness the parents must have to raise their other children, continue to work, and just get out of bed every day understanding what they will encounter, is beyond comprehension. The next time you think of giving up, consider the battle these parents are facing and the fact that they will fight for their children until the day they die.

You can muster the mental strength to do anything you put your mind to, but you cannot leave room for self-pity, self-doubt, or the what-ifs.

CHALLENGE YOURSELF: PERFORMING UNDER PRESSURE

Any elite athlete needs to be able to focus and perform under all circumstances. To maintain composure and perform at their peak, athletes must find ways to channel their thinking into a positive outcome.

Let's say you are presenting a major proposal at work and are, understandably, nervous. Focus your thoughts on what you do well and what you need to accomplish. If you're doing a large presentation at work, remind yourself of the following:

- You've done your research.

- You are good at public speaking.

- Your ideas are solid

- You are presenting to people who respect what you have to say.

- You are doing your best.

Take a deep breath, and focus your thoughts on the great job you will do because you have mentally prepared for this day. Remember, you only fail if you haven't tried.

KEY TAKEAWAYS

In this chapter, you learned about:

- Signs of mental toughness include the ability to self-monitor, accept the consequences of your actions, and let go of the past.

- Daily habits of mentally tough people are perseverance, hard work, and self-confidence.

- Use visualization techniques daily to help improve mental toughness. This includes picturing where you see yourself once your goal has been realized.

3

NEVER JUDGE MENTAL TOUGHNESS BY ITS COVER

Mental toughness and physical strength are completely different. A man can go to the gym and lift weights every day and be incredibly physically strong, prepared for any physical endurance test that is thrown at him, but that doesn't mean that he would be mentally prepared to deal with something of equal mental difficulty. A great expectation is that physically strong people can deal with anything that they face and that a physically weak person will fall apart at the slightest unhinging, but that is false.

To overcome adversity, one needs to be strong, but that's not possible for everyone. Most people can handle slight disruptions in their lives without falling apart, such as dealing with a difficult coworker, but it takes a mentally tough person to be able to overcome extreme situations or persevere through trying times.

The people that have risked their own health, time, and safety for others, may not look exceptional if you pass them on the street. They may look ordinary, weak even, on the outside, but if you were able to see inside their minds you would see the strength that is exuding within.

I have seen well-built men with loud personalities fall apart under stress and I have seen slight women who are typically not taken seriously, react to stressful situations with grace and strength. The ability to handle adversity and challenges in life has nothing to do with one's appearance so be careful not to judge mental toughness by its cover.

Are you someone who already shows promise of mental strength? Here's how to tell:

1. Confidence: A sign of mental toughness is to be confident in yourself and in your abilities to perform challenges you set

for yourself and in getting through difficult times. Every chance you get, practice being confident in yourself and remind yourself of all that you have done. If you are trying to beat a time in a marathon or climbing the ladder to your dream job, do what you need to do to reach those goals every day; practice makes perfect.

2. Maintain Your Calm: Everyone who exhibits mental toughness is capable of maintaining a calm attitude when things get stressful. Exhibiting mental strength is remaining chill and calm when everyone else is entering panic mode.

   Few people are born with the gift of calm in a chaotic situation; there is much practice that is needed. People who want to build mental toughness need to experience difficulties, within reason, so putting themselves in uncomfortable situations is necessary to build resilience or to be prepared for feared emergencies. If someone is afraid of their children choking, for instance, taking a first aid course and learning how to deal with these situations will help them to remain calm in a stressful situation. Someone that is intrigued by rock climbing but afraid of heights will need to begin with small cliffs and work up to higher climbs to build resilience.

3. Adversity in Life: Someone who has come through extreme adversity in life and had to deal with challenges that are not a normal part of life is mentally tough; they have to be. Overcoming racism, psychological or physical abuse, neglect, growing up in poverty, or other challenges gives you an insight that not everyone has. These challenges give a perception in life that it is possible to overcome tragedy and that small issues are not worth wasting time on.

When you have not grown up with obstacles in your life, you don't know what it means to fight to overcome adversity. This, of course, is not something one should be blamed for. We all dream of a life without complications, but it is only those who have had to climb out of the rubble of a broken life, rise above grief, or persevere beyond other opposition that will truly know what it takes to be mentally strong.

EXAMPLES OF THOSE WHO HAVE MENTAL TOUGHNESS

Mental toughness is necessary to thrive in life. There are some people who are expected, by society and their peers, to be mentally tough, but there are others who exude a quiet strength that many overlook.

In society, we often see the elderly, women, and children as weak—often at just a glance. Let's take Drew Barrymore as an example most of us recognize. Today she is a well-adjusted mom of two kids and has a successful talk show, as well as a booming movie production company—but her childhood would have broken most. She was interviewed (*Drew Barrymore*, 2021)and talked about growing up in Hollywood, surrounded by celebrities, and had her first movie break at age five in E.T. Drew was introduced to drugs at a party at age nine and quickly formed an addiction for which she went to rehab at age 12. She was then admitted to a mental facility by her mother at age 13 and was there for 18 months. She fought to be emancipated from her parents at age 14 and won. She has made a wonderful career for herself and has, with daily effort, fought to keep her sobriety.

Barrymore's journey is not something that many adults are mentally strong enough to deal with, but she managed to find the determination and perseverance to remove herself from a life that tried to kill her innocence.

Some other people we underestimate in regard to their mental toughness include:

- Those who give birth: Giving birth is one of the most excruciating events that one can go through. Not only does labor pose physical pain, but there is the psychological element that accompanies the process. She may not be muscular, but withstanding the pain of contractions and the worry of delivering a healthy child is something that most muscular men would not be able to endure. Without mental strength, childbirth would not occur and if not for the incredible mental toughness of those who go through labor, our species would die off. So the next time you see a slight woman with her little one, remember that they are here because of the mother's sheer strength.

- First responders: When you look through history and study the various disasters, wars, terror attacks, pandemics, and other pandamonium, there is one constant - the mental toughness of first responders. When the twin towers fell on September 11th, 2001 and people fled for their lives, stunned, not knowing what had happened, firefighters threw on their gear and ran into the immense black clouds of smoke and debris without a thought for themselves. The mental strength that any firefighter needs to have during a fire or other disaster is unfathomable. They put themselves in danger's way to save humans, pets, and what remains of treasured possessions.

- Medical professionals: Doctors and nurses show incredible mental toughness every day in their jobs but that was ten-fold during the Covid-19 pandemic when they showed us on a larger scale, the sacrifices they were willing to make for the well-being of others. It took incomprehensible mental toughness for medical staff to walk into a hospital and care for those who were not only dying of an unpredictable

223

disease but to do it while knowing full well they were putting themselves at risk of contracting this disease.

WHEN EXPECTATIONS EXCEED REALITY

Never let someone's appearance lure you into believing they are incapable of doing great things. Likewise, don't assume someone who is well-built and has extreme physical strength can handle emotionally charged or mentally anguished situations.

Remember that slight mom I just mentioned? Chances are she can handle tense situations and stress much better than the bodybuilder that spends hours a day at the gym. Lifting weights takes practice and makes you look intimidating, but size has nothing to do with mental toughness.

No matter your gender, size, or age, you are not born mentally tough but it can be earned and learned. It is not the physical girth of someone that makes an impression on this world, but the immense courage it takes for them to fight for what they want and to look at others with the respect that is earned.

The mind is the most powerful part of any one of us. It has the ability to break us or lead us to our ultimate goals. If you allow yourself to believe that someone who is 6-ft-3 is mentally stronger than a 5-foot-tall old woman, that's your assumption and chances are, it's the wrong one.

When you look at Holocaust survivors, many are frail women. These women speak of the children that were stolen from them, the spouses that were shot in front of them, and the torture that they endured. The only reason they are still alive is their own willpower, their own persistence, and their own strength.

To lose a child and carry on living is a great example of mental strength in itself, but to continue living a life where you can help others is a true testament of will. You may not realize it, but one of the most powerful women in the world is also one of the most mentally tough, yet the tragedies she's lived through might be too much for Captain America. This would be none other than Oprah Winfrey.

Oprah explains in her book, (What Happened, 2021) about the early years of her life. Born to a teenage mother, was raised in poverty and eventually sent to live with her grandmother who then raised her. At only age nine, she was sexually assaulted by a cousin. She was assaulted until she was 13 years old, and gave birth at age 14 to a baby boy who died when he was only two weeks old. It was through her child's death that Oprah decided to take back her life, build mental strength, and persevere to the powerhouse woman she is today.

CHALLENGE YOURSELF: BECOME RESILIENT

To build mental toughness, we must go through uncomfortable and challenging situations. To increase your resilience to the uncomfortable, try having a cold shower every morning. This exercise will help build your mental toughness due to physical and mental discomfort.

Taking cold showers helps boost our lymph circulation which helps increase our immune system and endocrine function which in turn helps increase proper blood circulation. A cold shower will help build resilience that will help you become more mentally tough (*Resilience: Build Skills*, n.d.).

KEY TAKEAWAYS

In this chapter, you learned that:

- mental toughness has no face. A child can exude more mental toughness than a grown man. Don't judge mental toughness by its cover.

- mental toughness is possessed by those who have faced adversity and challenges.

- a person who is mentally tough exudes confidence and can remain calm under stressful circumstances.

4

TODAY'S SOFTENED GENERATION

You may be hearing a lot of chatter and the accumulative sound of eye-rolling from older generations as they watch today's youth (and many middle-aged folks) clamor for recognition and sustainability from doing virtually nothing (Hogg, 2021).

Back in the day—particularly before social media took over the world—people had to work hard and get by on their own grit and determination to rise to the top and make a good living. There was a lot of competition and not everyone received a participation badge. Today's youth in particular seems to want it all dropped at their feet while they are live-streaming or dancing their exuberant yet vastly under-talented feet off.

Even the peers of those who feel entitled are seeking retribution for the bad name that has been bestowed upon all youth. There is a majority of today's generation that feel they should be given a free ride based on the fact that they are young and enthusiastic, but many born into Generation Y want to be recognized for their work ethic.

Today we are constantly slammed with the term *influencer* or *content creator*, which basically means their contribution to society is filming TikTok videos or doing make-up tutorials. While these may be entertaining to watch, today's *influencers* are not making any significant changes to our world and are actually making themselves mentally weak.

Exactly why are millennials so soft? Many would say it is due to parenting and the fact that many of today's youth are handed everything on a silver platter because they want their children not to suffer the difficulty of a hard day's work. Others blame society for making it so easy to get by with a wink and a smile. The real reasons that today's youth are so soft could be largely due to the following:

- Everything Comes Easy: It wasn't always easy growing up in the '70s, '80s, and '90s, but as parents, many have failed to provide the basic coping skills to their children. There's no doubt that many young adults today have received awards, own cars, and have more than the previous generation dreamed of, and it is well earned, but not by them. Rather, it was earned by their parents or other societal pressures that created a matrix of evaluations and situations whereby everyone needs to be recognized.

I am glad to have grown up in a time when you had to earn your worth, your validation, and your recognition. There are changes that need to be made by society and the young adults of today if they want to live a life they can be proud of truly earning, and one that won't disappear as they age.

- Everyone Wins–Even Without Trying: The ego of millennials has a thirst for attention that never seems quenched. It began for this generation with the parents who raised their children as peers and not as people they should say no to. At school, everyone gets a participation ribbon and there are no grades in elementary school but everyone gets a smiley face, gold star, or thumbs up. The times of there being one winner–a single excellence achiever–are gone and it is making for some young adults who have never been told no and have no idea how to actually vie for what they want.

- Validation Generation: Everyone seemingly needs validation in the form of likes or views when it comes to social media. From first dates, weddings, meals, or dance crazes, everyone seems to need validation for every little thing that they do. The days of quietly doing a good job and feeling good about yourself are gone and there are videos of people ordering coffee, live-streaming in Disneyland, and posting every aspect of their lives to be rated and affirmed. The true sadness lies in the fact that with constant posting and pleading for recognition, the ability to enjoy the small moments and feel proud of achievements is lost in the shuffle to seek out others' opinions.

- Expect Wealth for Average work: Working nine to five may allow you to make enough money to get by, but it won't make you rich. Today's youth expect to go to an average job, do average work, and live a good life without budgeting. There have been videos posted by employees at popular coffee chains, restaurants, and other positions that are reacting to a 30-hour week as though they were being held hostage without food or bathroom breaks for that time. Millennials say they can change the world, solve world hunger, and house the poor, but they also expect to do this by filming homeless people shivering while they stare through a lens. Without doing much of anything, they expect adoration and recognition.

- Role Models Are Famous for the Wrong Reasons: Having someone to look up to is fine, but there is a difference between commending the passion of Greta Thunburg or the philanthropic endeavors of Princess Diana and celebrating and idolizing the random "icons" who became popular overnight. Rather than seeking out the issues of the world and trying to make it a better place, by becoming educated on climate change for instance, millennials would rather spend their time streaming YouTube and concerning themselves with who the newest Hollywood star is, maybe dating.

The generalization is that Generation Y is consumed with being validated by others and recognized and praised for things that literally anyone can do with a ring light and script. In the Olympics you don't get a medal just for showing up, yet that's what elementary schools are introducing to our youth. With the expectation that everyone wins for no reason, no wonder we are seeing an influx of youth expecting success to be handed to them on a silver platter.

Society did today's youth no favors by coddling them for the slightest inconveniences and for rewarding them for what should be expected of them. Imagine your boss gave you a raise for all your hard work, but you knew you had been slacking off for the last two weeks. Would you feel that you needed to put in the effort to be rewarded? Of course not! The same message is being sent to youth when they receive accolades for work they haven't done. They expect praise for nothing. There is no need to put in effort to get a reward that you are receiving for doing nothing and the drive will be gone to prove them right.

WHAT IS WRONG WITH NEEDING ATTENTION

It's nice to feel appreciated but constantly vying for notoriety, especially when there is no valid reason, promotes emotional instability and mental weakness. Needing to be validated by others to do anything is a detriment to self-value and worth (Litner, n.d.).

Increasingly, millennials are engaging in sharing private moments of themselves or others and expect others to feel anguish at disheartening moments and to become emotionally invested. Some *influencers* are so convinced that their followers will be distraught without their posts that they make a whole blog or video on how they need to take a break to regain their mental health. While focusing on mental toughness is key to living a successful life, building your whole world on a very public platform is the opposite of having mental strength.

There is an abundance of people who post about or discuss their struggles with finances, relationships, or jobs and eat up the pity that anyone throws in their direction. Their ego is fed, not by the satisfaction they get out of a hard day's work, but by the hollow accolades they receive from people that they often don't even know.

When we seek the comfort or praise of others to feel worth something, we become less mentally tough. Without self-worth that grows organically from hard work, sacrifice, failure, and success, we are not going to gain strength. We gain mental toughness from working through our difficulties and taking accountability for our mistakes, not blaming them on others. We only learn from what we have done wrong if we acknowledge those mistakes and take responsibility for them. It does nothing to brush issues to the side and blame others for what we have become.

There are different types of validation that affect our mental toughness very differently: internal and external validation. Here's the difference (Streefkerk, 2019).

- Internal validation: The feelings of validation that you have toward yourself and your feelings, allowing them to be recognized and accepted. Internal validation means that you give accolades to your efforts and feel comfortable and confident in who you are so that outside judgment and criticism do not bring you down.

- External validation: This is the reliance on the support and opinions of others to validate your worth. You may find it difficult to do much without the encouragement and support of others pushing you forward.

Seeking support or validation from an external source is okay, as long as it does not control feelings we have about our worth. There is a spectrum of validation that people require from outside sources and many are not going to harm your mental toughness, but there are some that rely on external validation, which is very damaging to the psyche and causes mental weakness.

WHY DO PEOPLE SEEK EXTERNAL VALIDATION?

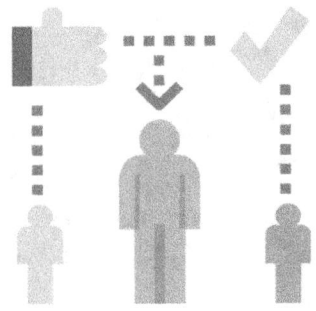

There are many reasons that someone may rely on external validation from others. These reasons include gaining a feeling of self-worth, how you rely on others, and may affect how you act around others.

I believe those who received emotional validation from their parents at a young age have a greater sense of security and emotional cognizance. A child that is given praise and a feeling of worth will grow up feeling that she or he is capable of doing great things.

From my experience, when children are raised in an environment that is devoid of encouragement, depriving them of self-worth, they are less likely to have the ability to regulate emotions. These children may also have difficulty with or be susceptible to the following:

233

- inability to trust other people

- fear of being rejected

- chronic anxiety

- arbitrary behavior

Studies have linked mental health conditions such as borderline personality disorder or depression, to growing up in an environment where you were not validated.

On the other side, excessive validation and praise can cause children to grow up with a feeling of entitlement and superiority which may make it challenging to have meaningful relationships or relate to others. With constant praise comes a narcissistic personality that can transpire into issues later in life, such as

- body dysmorphic disorder.

- histrionic personality disorder.

- dependent personality disorder.

Not everyone that has experienced excessive praise as children will have these personality traits, but it may resonate with you, in which case, it is a good thing you have this book to help set you on the path toward mental toughness.

ARE YOU SOMEONE WHO SEEKS VALIDATION?

The balance between internal validation and external validation can shift to an unhealthy balance quickly. Sharing your good news with family and friends is not necessarily a bad thing, but how do you know if you've gone too far to the external validation side?

You may be at risk of needing too much external validation if you do any of the following:

- You have a difficult time setting boundaries

- You find yourself being an overachiever for the praise of others

- You feel guilty saying no

- You avoid conflict

- You take rejection, such as not getting a job promotion, personally

- You post provocative content online for attention

- You feel that you must know everything to be liked

- You gossip constantly to get attention

- You agree to do things you don't want to do so others will like you

- You exaggerate a circumstance to gain notoriety or attention

- You become distressed when attention shifts away from you

- Your quest to gain outside approval becomes all-consuming

- Your view shifts when someone doesn't agree with you

There are many people-pleasing aspects to someone who is seeking external validation and several habits that will lower self-esteem and create rifts between relationships. Becoming mentally tough is going to help heal some of these negative aspects of your life and help you become a more successful and strong-willed individual.

Seeking validation from others steals the power you should be giving to yourself and lends it to someone else, giving them ultimate control over how you feel about yourself. You should never allow anyone else to validate you other than yourself because it steals from what you think you are capable of.

Running to someone else any time you feel you might be making the wrong decision or to see if you are doing a good job only takes away the internal validation you should be giving to yourself as someone who is building mental toughness.

EXERCISES TO STOP SEEKING EXTERNAL VALIDATION

You may have been well aware that you sought validation from others or maybe you have only realized it through reading the last section of this chapter, but either way it needs to stop.

We feel good about receiving accolades for a job well done, and we should, but it should only enhance our pride—not be dependent on it. Someone who thrives on external validation, such as the TikTok influencers mentioned above, demonstrates a lack of self-worth and an absence of mental toughness.

There are a variety of ways you can stop this negative behavior.

1. Explore Your Childhood: Rediscover your childhood and identify different situations or people who may have made you feel invalidated. Did you feel unheard or unattended as a child? What were the situations in which you felt neglected or that you deserved praise that was never given? Some call this exploring your inner child and by doing so, you can discover many things that you were never provided with that are essential to healthy self-esteem and mental strength.

    Once you determine what you never received as a child, whether it be attention, compassion, or praise, then you can begin to give yourself all of those things that you were lacking. As an example, if you did not get praise for working hard as a child, tell yourself often that you are doing a good job and have worked hard to make it as far as you are.

2. Say No: Seeking external validation and doing whatever will please other people is a difficult thing to stop, especially when you are afraid of losing people as a result. Don't worry, you don't have to go cold turkey, but you do need to make baby steps right away.

   Begin by saying no to little things and deal with small amounts of discomfort before moving onto a larger scale of rejecting others. Eventually, you will be more comfortable refusing larger asks, especially when you realize that not everyone—very few in fact—will turn away when they are refused.

3. Practice Self-Validation: Rather than reaching out to others to validate feelings of worth, practice self-validating techniques that empower you. Positive affirmations can help replace negative feelings and self-talk that only serves to debilitate your self-esteem. Remind yourself through self-affirmations that you are enough and that you are capable.

4. Connect with Mentally Strong People: Take a hard look at your support network and consider if they are supportive or if they contribute to codependent behaviors. Does your network support strong ideas and encourage you to work harder or do they encourage you to dwell on the negative and suffocate you with their own issues? A strong support network will support your boundaries and encourage you on the path to success.

5. Deconstruct Negative Relationships: Seeking external validation once in a while to celebrate your accomplishments is okay, but do the people you are

reaching out to have your best interests at heart, or are they likely to exploit your personal traumas?

Anyone who will turn your difficulties into their own personal discussions or use them against you is not someone you want in your corner. Internal validation is key to giving you the drive to succeed that you need.

There is a spectrum to external validation. Asking for someone to join in your celebratory moments or asking for advice occasionally is one thing but when it becomes a constant way to seek validation, you need to seek other options for empowerment. Seek internal validation for your accomplishments and take accountability for mistakes and learn from them moving forward.

CHALLENGE YOURSELF: INITIATE A DIFFICULT CONVERSATION

There are times in life when we must decide to have a difficult conversation with someone we have in our personal or work life. Often, people tend to tiptoe around sensitive topics and avoid bringing up conversations that can initiate unfavorable or difficult outcomes.

You may have someone in your life that exhibits many of the traits that are listed in this chapter. Maybe your sister is always on social media, posting everything about her life and everyone else's and it's made you feel uncomfortable and a bit annoyed. Take the opportunity to sit down with her and discuss how this makes you feel and let her know that you don't want your life spattered across social media for all to see. Her life being a free-for-all is her decision, but it does not apply to you.

If you have a boss that constantly makes you stay late while they leave early several times a week, have that difficult conversation. If running the business as though it were your own is not something you agreed to, it is up to you to have that difficult conversation with them and let them know that it needs to stop.

With any situation that requires that difficult talk, stick to your guns and accept the consequences that come.

KEY TAKEAWAYS:

Throughout this chapter, you learned:

- The expectations of today's youth exceed their accomplishments.

- People crave external validation because they don't believe in themselves. Practice telling people 'no,' practice self-validation, and connect to mentally strong people to avoid seeking external validation.

- Build up your self-worth to build internal validation by giving yourself credit for what you have accomplished, and acknowledging the validity of your feelings.

5

MENTAL TOUGHNESS COMES FROM DOING THE HARD THINGS OVER AND OVER AGAIN

We are blessed to live in an era busting with technological advances, quick weight loss fixes, and recognition for virtually nothing. Convenience has made life easier in many respects but it has also contributed to complacency, especially in the younger generations that were born into this accommodating age. We have already discussed, in the previous chapter, how today's generation receives recognition too easily and without having to try at all, never mind repeatedly.

In a pinch, most people will take advantage of the easy way out, but the issue today is that rather than that road being the least traveled, it is downtrodden and broken from overuse. It seems that most people want to put in the least effort to make it big in life and reap the rewards of hard work that they don't necessarily want to put in.

The recognition that many seek via social media is a great example of doing little with the expectation that great things should be received. Posting a 3-minute video harping about someone that ruined your customer experience or posting a verse of a song expecting to be the next Taylor Swift is not realistic. The trouble with today's society is that everyone expects to succeed with minimal effort.

Mental toughness is built through trial and error, dedication to hard work for desired results, and not giving up despite the turmoil. There is very little worth having that comes from little effort and everything worth going for will come from determination and grit.

Getting a promotion requires you to spend extra hours in the office well after others have gone home. Graduating at the top of your class means doing extra research on a term paper or studying for an exam well after you feel comfortable with the material. Losing weight is more than popping pills or starving yourself; it is about exercising regularly and feeding your body with the necessary nutrients to flourish.

Going the easy route will only make you reliant on other people or on supplements, but putting in the work necessary to achieve great results on your own will help you build mental toughness. Through failure and resurrection, you will become reliant on yourself and grow confidence in your abilities to get things done. No one that has earned their success has ever gone the easy route and those who have clawed their way to the top have shared common traits.

A large part of what makes someone mentally tough is resilience. Being able to deal with difficult situations such as relationship issues, financial distress, or health issues is what makes someone resilient. Just as we can build our mental toughness, resilience is built up of different situations that we overcome. It is the ability to thrive amid adversity and the ongoing perseverance that one shows.

We don't all consciously become resilient—in fact, it's not often something we set out to do. Some people are thrust into challenging their toughness due to a circumstance or occurrence that they never imagined could happen to them.

For example, a young mother who visits the doctor with a complaint that she is exhausted from caring for her children finds out that she actually has cancer, and this is the cause of her energy depletion. This is not a scenario that a happy young mother imagines, but it's now something that she needs to deal with. Accepting that this is your place in life is not easy. In fact, it builds mental toughness. Fighting the disease that is trying to steal your life is what builds resilience.

Another example that haunts me is the families that were forever changed after the terrorist attack on September 11th. There were many people that were challenged and rose to the occasion of becoming resilient through extreme trauma and change, including spouses who lost the loves of their lives, parents who lost children, and children who lost parents. Those left behind had to pick up the pieces of their lives and work through the emotions that were forced upon them. Everyone affected by that day that lived to tell about it was challenged and had to adapt to their feelings of loss, fear, and anger. None of those people set out to be mentally strong that day, but all of them needed to be and they rose to the challenge through struggle, hard work, and perseverance of a determined spirit to not let evil win.

COMMON TRAITS OF MENTALLY TOUGH PEOPLE

As mentioned previously, no one is born with mental toughness; it has to be earned through hard work, failure, resilience, and reliance on one's self. As with myself, you may find your true calling through perseverance and resilience. Using the building blocks of a failed endeavor will construct a deeper meaning with a stronger foundation.

Those who build mental strength do have common traits built on habits that they practice each day (Cikanavicius & Juby, 2017).

1. Challenge themselves: Mentally strong individuals seek amends for their mistakes rather than slink into hiding. They grow from their missteps and view obstacles as a way to better themselves.

2. Focus on situations they can control: Mentally strong people will focus their energy on things that they can impact and control. They will not waste time worrying about events that cannot be altered but will hone in on what they can alter or what makes them feel empowered.

3. Set clear and achievable goals: They set goals that are clear and attainable and strive to reach them each day. They get up in the morning with a set structure of what they need to accomplish and focus their energy on reaching these milestones.

4. Champions of change: Those who are mentally strong are thrust into constant adaptation, especially those in roles of leadership, so they need to be flexible. These individuals often have contingency plans in place for the possibility of future change that may occur within a company, establishment, political party, or another leadership vessel.

5. Use failure to catapult to success: Anyone in a position of power, and individuals who have done well in their chosen path, know that success is reached through trial and error. Small mistakes are used by mentally tough people to learn from and to turn into greater potential moving forward. There is a risk of failure in everything we do and not all of our endeavors will be successful ones but it is what we do with failure that truly leads to success.

6. Dissolution of fear. Fear leads to missed opportunities and stunts the fire that could be used to thrust us toward our dreams. Many people put off changing jobs, asking for a raise, pitching an idea, going on a trip, and truly living their lives because they are afraid to fail. We all must seek our dreams and then make them happen so that our list of regrets is limited to what we couldn't do, not because of a lack of trying, but because we needed to amend our path.

7. Exude confidence: When you are confident, you are more likely to try new things and rise to the challenge of tasks that are more intricate or difficult for others to try. When you exude confidence, others believe that you can take charge and are trustworthy to do what needs to be done,

therefore you are more likely to be chosen for a job, as part of a team, or as a go-to person for your boss.

8. Receiving constructive criticism: When you are mentally tough, you are able to handle constructive criticism well and utilize the advice to make things better. If you get insulted when someone gives you feedback on your performance, practice listening and digesting the comments. You don't have to follow all advice, but listening to what others have to say will open you up to a world of good.

9. Practice dismissing toxic people: It is challenging to exclude people from your life, especially family members or friends that you have relied on for your whole life, but there comes a time when you need to consider if these people really have your back. When someone puts down one of your ideas without any helpful advice or shows remorse for your good fortune, practice walking away from that relationship or at the very least, limiting your contact with that individual. Mentally tough people surround themselves with positive and like-minded individuals, not those who create drama.

10. Work with adversity: True mental strength is derived from overcoming adversity rather than succumbing to it. When something seems insurmountable, take the initiative to work your way around that problem or find another way. Transform an adverse circumstance into a forcefield of energy.

We are all going to face obstacles in our lives, whether they are brought on by circumstance or by what we set out to accomplish. Following through on our ideals and pushing onward despite challenges that seem to be hopeless is what being mentally tough is all about.

GRADUAL PROGRESS IS STILL PROGRESS

When you are beginning to overcome a challenge, you need to start slowly to avoid feeling overwhelmed and giving in altogether. It's okay to build up to things over time, as long as you stick to it and don't renege on your obligations to others and yourself.

Some examples of things you can work up to gradually include

- working out 5 days a week.

- beginning a calorie-deficit diet.

- going back to school to change a career or expand current knowledge.

WORKING OUT

When you have never exercised before or don't do so on a regular basis, it can seem overwhelming to engage in physical activity multiple days per week. To increase your chances of success, determine your goals and build from there, whether it be weight loss, training for a triathlon, or getting fit for life.

Say your goal is to work out five days a week so that you can become fitter. You are going to exhaust yourself and fatigue your muscles if you go hard from day one, and from zero to five days is not realistic. Instead, set a time limit for when you want to be at your optimal goal of five days a week and then build from there.

For example:

- Goal: Working out five days per week within one month

- Week 1: Work out Monday, and Wednesday

- Week 2: Work out Monday, Wednesday, and Friday

- Week 3: Workout Monday, Tuesday, Thursday, and Friday

- Week 4: Workout Monday, Tuesday, Thursday, Friday, and Saturday

Setting clear and attainable goals will help you reach your ultimate destination without feeling overwhelmed or like you are failing.

CALORIE-DEFICIT DIET

If you want to lose weight, you need to reduce calorie consumption so that the calories you consume during the day do not exceed the calories you expel (Frysh, 2021). Cutting calories too much right off the bat will lead to hunger and other adverse effects that could result in you giving up your goal altogether. Instead, if you are planning on lowering your caloric intake from 2100 to 1800 per day, do so little by little. For example:

- Week 1: Cut 100 calories per day

- Week 2: Cut 200 calories per day

- Week 3: Cut 300 calories per day

By the end of the 3rd week, you will be down to your optimal calorie intake and it will have been gradual enough that you won't have felt hungry or that you are giving up too much.

GOING BACK TO SCHOOL

Some jobs require that you keep up to date on current statistics, styles, or curriculum, or you may even want to change your career altogether. Going back to school can be expensive and time-consuming which makes it an unlikely resource for anyone who has significant financial obligations, but it isn't impossible for those who are capable and willing to put in the work.

If you are upgrading a degree or changing careers altogether, there are several courses available online and most can be done in your own time frame so you are not giving up your main source of income while you better your chances of making more money. If you take a course or study for a career change online, make sure you set out specific times that you will work on your studies so that you don't push them until later in the day and then run out of time altogether. Having a set schedule will help keep you on track.

Progress is progress, and some people are able to get to their goals quicker than others, depending on a variety of factors, including:

- Financial obligations such as providing for their family

- Personal responsibilities such as children

No matter what obligations you have in life, you are going to get to your end game if you have a plan and determination. Setting a deadline for when you want to complete your schooling, open your business, or change careers, will help you keep a steady pace in developing your ideas and reaching your planned opportunity in a timely manner. Not setting a deadline can prolong the time it takes to reach the outcome since there would be no time limit, which often leads to procrastination.

CHALLENGE YOURSELF: WHAT WAS YOUR MOMENT?

This may be difficult to address, especially if you have put the past to rest, but think of what initially gave you the knowledge that you were mentally tough or what will catapult you from tragedy to triumph?

Most people who search for mental toughness or that have gained mental strength, have dealt with adversity, trauma, or another painful situation that has introduced a need to gain strength or collapse into themselves.

What was the moment that made you strong? Did you go through a divorce? Were you severely injured and needed to claw your way back to health? Did you lose a loved one too soon in your life and struggle to carry on? It doesn't matter if it was hard or if you felt pain; all that is normal. What does matter is that you didn't wallow in self-pity and you dug yourself out of a difficult time and rose to the challenge of carrying on.

KEY TAKEAWAYS

In this chapter, you learned about:

- Gaining recognition and finding success without trying is what makes today's younger generation soft.

- Mentally tough people share common traits, such as using their mistakes to learn, challenging themselves, exuding confidence, and working through adversity.

- For success, you must set a goal and move mountains to get there.

6

YOU HAVE TO CHOOSE YOUR HARD

Life is a series of challenging and difficult tasks, decisions, and events, no matter which path we choose (Meinschein, n.d.). It's up to each chapterindividual to determine what hard means to them. It can be way more difficult to live with the consequences of being broke/unhealthy than to put in the effort to become successful/healthy. In other words, the price you will pay for not making your dreams come true is far greater than the one you will pay if you do.

Hard work goes into building a solid career that pays well, owning a beautiful house, and raising a family. You cannot take time to slack off or someone who is harder working will step in and take over with their work ethic. It is a decision that you make every day to work hard to live a good life.

You can thrive and live your best life or accept the *easy* way out and struggle in this life. Believe it or not, there is difficulty required for both of these paths, but only one allows you to reap the rewards of prosperity and mental strength.

THE DIFFICULT BUT PROSPEROUS PATH

There has to be a plan to follow the path that leads to prosperity and mental toughness. You cannot go out into the world hoping for the best and expecting it to happen without putting any forethought into it.

It's typical of human nature to follow the path of least resistance, but that path is crowded and worn down and leads to the same place as everyone else who settles for mediocrity. But if you are eager to thrive then there are some ways you can travel along the path to success.

1. Why is it difficult: What part of what you set out to do is difficult? Do not tell yourself that it is impossible because there is nothing that cannot be done without determination. Figure out what is difficult and then go about doing the things that can be done more efficiently so that by the time you get to the really hard part, you can see the goal line.
2. Go step by step: Often, when we think of something that needs to be done, we consider the end result and do not take the time to acknowledge that one larger task is only something that is obtained by taking several smaller steps. Instead of looking at the big picture, decide what you need to do one bit at a time so that the task feels much more doable.

3. Know your end game: What do you want to walk away with at the end of the day, task, or event? Know what that looks like. If your goal is to own a coffee shop, you can't just rent a building, throw in some coffee machines, and expect it to flourish. First, you need to draw up a business plan and have a clear idea of what you want your business to look like and how you will help it grow.

If you want to run a triathlon, you are not going to show up the day of the event and expect to finish in record time or without shin splints. You will need to set out a training schedule and build up your stamina and strength.

When you choose to go after what you want in life, you will need to work hard for it and continue to work hard to keep what you have earned. Anything worth having does not fall into one's lap, but is earned through a continuously strong work ethic and mental toughness.

THE DIFFICULTY OF CHOOSING THE EASY PATH

There is actually nothing easy about not putting the effort into yourself or your future. When you don't put in the effort to eat healthily and take care of your body, you are leading yourself down a path that will lead to health problems such as heart disease, diabetes, and obesity, which leads to a host of other issues. When people do not take care of themselves, they are essentially limiting their potential by allowing their bodies to become neglected and wither away.

When someone chooses to ignore their physical health. It may be easy to go through a drive-through for dinner on a busy day, or not exercise at all because setting an exercise routine is too difficult, you are denying yourself the basic needs of your body. When we don't eat well and take in the proper macronutrients that our bodies need, we are limiting our potential. Exercising and eating healthy support many necessities of life, such as:

- Good sleep patterns

- Emotional wellness

- Stabilizing moods

- Providing ample energy

- Lowering the risk of chronic diseases

- Cognitive clarity

- Sharpened decision-making skills

Your future will reflect the effort you have put into it. If you work hard, you will be more likely to have financial stability than if you put in minimal effort to just get by.

TURNING YOUR HARD INTO A FUTURE

Determining your future is one of the most difficult decisions you will ever make. What will it look like? What will you do? Will you work for someone else or will you start a business and be your own boss? No matter which path you choose, it will be difficult in varying ways.

Someone that chooses to work while upgrading a career will need to put in great effort and time management skills to ensure their future will lead to greater things. By working hard by day to pay the bills and putting themselves through school and attending school and doing homework by night, the hard work that is chosen will lead to a prosperous future. That is the hard thing they chose.

On the other hand, someone that doesn't want to work more than they have to might have a job that just pays the bills. But when the time comes to pay for an emergency, such as car repairs or medical bills, or if they are laid off due to lack of job security and have no savings, their hard will come in the form of trying to pay the bills, possibly taking out a payday or personal loan that they can't pay back and finding themselves falling deeper into debt. That is the hard thing they chose.

If you want to start your own business, you need to take into account all of the factors that go into that decision, such as determining:

- What type of business will it be?

- What will make it unique?

- How will others be able to identify your brand?

- What is your business structure?

- How will you market your business?

- Who is your customer base?

- What are your start-up costs?

- Will you take out a loan or will you get investors?

- Where will you open your business?

- How many employees will you need?

- Where will you get your supplies or products from?

You will also need to determine your accounts, brand, distribution, marketing, competitors, accounting, and other factors that go into running a business.

If you would rather be an employee, then you have other factors to consider, such as whether you go into a field that allows you to climb the ladder or a profession like teaching where you will happily sit for the rest of your career. Deciding to be a lawyer, teacher, doctor, electrician, or work in retail, all require different types of hard work. You need to decide which hard you are willing to embrace and then give it your all.

No matter what you choose to do with your career or yourself, it should be hard because you should be putting your entire effort into it. Life isn't easy no matter what path you choose, but it can be more rewarding depending on what you put into it and the mental strength you gain along the way.

HOW DIFFICULT IS YOUR CHOICE

Without thinking about it, we all choose our paths in life, work, and love. If you find yourself in a situation where you feel worthless, it might be time to ask yourself a few questions. Just remember that the grass may look greener on the other side of the office, in someone else's yard, or across the world, but what is it that you are genuinely ready to work hard for?

Is it time to switch jobs? Ask yourself some questions, such as are you excited about work or do you dread going in every morning?

- Is your work affecting you on personal time?

- Are others noticing that you are not happy in your job?

- Are your ideas dismissed at your work?

- Is it difficult to make ends meet based on your wage or salary?

- Has your mind been wandering to thoughts of another job?

Leaving a job that is not fulfilling is hard, but so is staying at a job that makes you feel like you are getting nowhere. Which hard are you willing to commit to based on the questions above?

Are you in a relationship that is stripping you of self-esteem? It takes a great deal of mental strength to leave a relationship, but it is just as difficult to stay in a commitment that is not going anywhere. If you feel you need to put your relationship into question, consider if it's time to leave your relationship:

- Does your partner submit you to physical or emotional abuse?

- Does your partner have a history of deceit?

- Has your partner been unfaithful?

- Does your partner see you as someone who has value?

- Is there mutual respect between you and your partner?

- Have you experienced feelings of unfulfillment in your relationship?

- Is there more give than take between either one of you?

- Is a lot expected of you in your relationship? Do you expect a lot?

When there is an imbalance in any relationship, whether platonic or romantic, there are going to be issues. While relationships take work every day, they should not be continually one-sided or make you feel as though you are missing out on something better.

CHANGE YOUR PATH

You need to reevaluate if you are struggling, whether it's with weight, your job, family and friends, or just life. If the struggles you are going through right now offer no reward at the end of it all, you need to consider if all the effort is worth it or if you should change your path.

For example, changing a job or making a career change is difficult, but if you are not happy where you are currently, or if you are barely paying the bills, or have two jobs to get by, then you need to consider changing your work. It's not easy to go to school and work to pay the bills but neither is working exhaustively for very little reward.

One of these difficult choices leads to years of struggle with no end in sight while the other will be challenging for a time, but there will be a goal and a deadline for you to begin seeing improvements in your finances and your mental state.

CHALLENGE YOURSELF EXERCISE: ARE YOU ON THE RIGHT PATH?

The great thing about life is that we can always change our direction in life if we aren't satisfied with where we are headed. Many people know the path they are meant to be on early in life while others struggle to find exactly where they belong.

To determine if you are on the right path to living your best life, ask yourself the following questions:

1. Are you happy in your job or career?

2. Have you decided to only have relationships with those who you respect and who respect you?

3. Are you setting new and more beneficial habits for yourself?

4. Do you often reevaluate your life?

5. Is there something that you look forward to?

Consider the answer to these questions and see if you need to make any adjustments so that you can answer yes to them all.

KEY TAKEAWAYS:

In this chapter, you learned that:

- The difficulties in chasing your dreams are far more rewarding than the grief of not trying at all.

- Your path to fulfillment and happiness should be through hard work and perseverance.

- When you doubt the path you are on, ask yourself if you are happy, content, and fulfilled.

7

THINGS YOU NEED TO BE AWARE OF WHEN YOU'RE STRUGGLING

An unsettling part of life is that we all go through adversity, but it's how you handle that adversity that sets you apart. Mental strength is the difference between accepting that challenges help shape who we are versus giving in to them and letting them weigh us down.

It is easy to feel that you are alone and that no one else has ever felt exactly as you do now (Costas & Denney, n.d.). There are many marginalized groups that, understandably, feel they are never going to find the support they need. Some of these groups include:

- members of the LGBTQIA+ community

- people going through divorce

- parents who have lost a child

- immigrants struggling to adjust to a new country

- victims of domestic violence

- those who struggle with clinical depression

Going through something life-altering makes someone feel isolated and it can be too painful for them to reach out. When you are struggling in life, it helps to remember that you are not alone in your journey of pain or disappointment. Everyone goes through victories and losses, which is what makes this life so precarious and wonderful. While it would be wonderful for everyone to flourish and for there to be no pain in this world, the fact is that for all our planning, we still have moments where we struggle.

Things you need to be aware of when you're struggling include

1. No One's Life is Without Sadness: Life is imperfect no matter who you are or how much you have. It's important to remember that the darkness you are going through right now is not going to last forever and that happiness is inevitable.

2. You Won't Always Struggle: Whatever you are going through right now, will pass. Whether you are going through financial difficulty, are arguing with a spouse, or arguing with friends, it won't always be this way.

3. You Don't Need to Suffer Alone: Reaching out to a family member or trusted friend when you are going through something serious in your life does not mean you are weak. It is okay to ask for help or have someone listen to what you need to get off your chest.

4. Acknowledge Your Feelings: Whatever you are feeling, no matter how unpleasant, acknowledge those feelings and what they mean to you. If you ignore how you are feeling, you will only make things worse later on as they will resurface. Giving your feelings a place will help keep them from coming back later on.

5. Turn Your Struggles Into a Lesson: Using your struggles as an opportunity to learn and grow is a stellar move. Most successful people built their empires on the stepping stones of mistakes and struggles throughout their journey.

6. Acknowledge All That You Have: It is easy to become bogged down with the negative in life and overlook all that we have. To remind yourself that these struggles are temporary, write down in a notebook, every day, all that you have to be thankful for so that you have a visual of how blessed you truly are.

7. Switch Your Mindset: The struggles you are going through are valid, but when we focus too much on the negative we can feel that what we are going through is insurmountable. Knowing your struggles and making a plan to move beyond them is productive. But fixating on these issues is only going to make things worse.

8. Everything Happens For a Reason: We may not understand what it is, but everything happens for a reason. Every challenge presents an opportunity for growth and change for the better, but sometimes we have to create the reason ourselves. As long as we don't dwell on the negatives in life, we can embrace the highs and lows of our every day that make life as memorable as it is. It is an unrealistic expectation for everything to always go as planned, so take the challenge and turn it into success.

9. Your Struggles Are Valid: It can be disheartening, and even annoying when you are expressing your challenges and someone takes it upon themselves to express their own journey. It is expected that if you share your experiences, others will do the same, but it's important to remember that your issues are valid, no matter what someone else's experiences may be. The important thing is not to dwell on what we are struggling with while also giving them the validation they deserve.

ANY OBSTACLE CAN BE OVERCOME

With few exceptions, all obstacles can be overcome. There can be impediments that lead to a dead-end street in one avenue of your path, but there is always a way around it. Find a solution that will act as a bridge to get you back on the right track to where you need to be. For some, this may be delaying progress in opening their restaurant because of a hold-up with the building contractor. This does not mean that all is lost, it gives one more time to prepare for when the day arrives and possibly get other things done that they were going to wait to do.

The first step to overcoming obstacles is to identify them and absolve them. If you do not take the opportunity to acknowledge any impediment, you may

- feel frustrated that good fortune evades you and someone else always gets the same good luck.

- experience overwhelming thoughts that you will fail until you believe it.

- have feelings of inadequacy that you could have done better if you did not lack the ability, intelligence, or conviction.

- feel jealous and angry that others are thriving while you struggle.

266

- find that stress has a significant negative effect on your mental wellness.

- experience conversations that loop in your head about what you think you can achieve and wish others would know.

Taking these few examples of how succumbing to obstacles can affect your life, learn what to avoid and use the following strategies to overcome obstacles and become more mentally tough and successful.

DEFINING YOUR OBSTACLE

Is your obstacle a perception or reality? No obstacle is insurmountable, yet our minds often make us believe that they are. Our minds often warp the severity of the obstacle depending on our current mental state, position in life, and how many obstacles we have overcome.

If you have recently dealt with an emotional blow, such as a friend being rude to you, then being rejected for a raise or promotion may seem very personal when it is not. If the same rejection came at a time when everything in your life was going well, perhaps it wouldn't seem like such a blow to your ego. We often perceive the severity of an obstacle based on what we already have going on at the moment.

CHANGING HOW YOU PERCEIVE YOURSELF

Often, obstacles begin with our lack of self-confidence and what we believe we do and don't deserve. When you believe many of the challenges in your life come from within, it means you have a negative view of yourself. This way of thinking needs to change.

Make a list of all the words you would use to describe yourself, then cross off any negative words that you have written down. Moving forward, think of yourself in the positive light of your own words, without any of the negative. The first step to overcoming obstacles is believing that you can and if you think ill of yourself, you aren't going to have much of a chance. You need to know that you are capable of moving beyond what is holding you back.

BELIEVING IN YOURSELF

People are often afraid to move beyond the rut they are stuck in because they don't believe they can do better or they do not deserve better. Overcoming obstacles is going to happen when you envision what you want and believe that you can get there.

If you want a better job, a house with a picket fence, or to travel around the world, envision yourself there and then make the small steps it takes to get to that point.

SETTING CLEAR, ATTAINABLE, AND MANAGEABLE GOALS

I have discussed goals previously, and we are going to discuss them again. Taking steps toward your goals is critical, but to get there you need a map of where you want to end up. The goals you set need to be clear to you and those around you so that there is no abandoning them. You may need to be redirected occasionally or take a step or two back, but the path to what you want should always be marked. Other ways to reach your goals include:

- State them clearly: Say you want to become more self-aware, for example.

- Make them achievable: Set goals that can be achieved, not ones that are so far-fetched you will not be able to attain them. An achievable goal would be to make more money within the year. An almost unattainable goal would be to become a millionaire in the next year when you have $100 in your bank account.

- Make them measurable: Rather than saying you want to lose weight, say how much weight you want to lose and then set a timeline for when that goal will become a reality.

There are some life-altering obstacles that no one can go through unscathed, such as the death of a loved one, divorce, or the loss of a job. Understandably, these losses can make one feel hopeless. It is also through these obstacles that people find their true mental strength and rise to new levels of determination. Many will turn their devastation into a way of motivating others to overcome their challenges.

MENTAL STRENGTH IS USING ADVERSITY TO BUILD SUCCESS

Impossibility is not in the vocabulary of someone who has built up their mental toughness. There are many examples of people you know to be successful now, but who at one point faced insurmountable odds only to come back stronger than ever.

WILLIE NELSON

Few country artists are as beloved as American country music icon, Willie Nelson, who has achieved accolades for over 60 decades. According to Forbes (Erb, n.d.), Nelson ran into trouble with the IRS after his accountants failed to pay his taxes properly for years.

After his financial downfall, Nelson took any job that he could, including a commercial for H&R Block, and managed to pay his debt to the IRS. He continues to record and tour, gaining popularity as one of the most popular country artists to this day.

MARTHA STEWART

On the Today Show (Kim, 2017), Martha Stewart opened up about some of her experiences, including prison. Martha Stewart worked her way through college. She is now an author, a home and garden icon, and she partners with Snoop Dogg on *Marth and Snoop's Potluck Dinner Party*. One of the most poignant aspects of Martha's life is that she became the world's first self-made billionaire all on her own.

Martha's namesake company went on the stock market in 1999, but only five years later, she was arrested and convicted of conspiracy in the case of ImCone. She was in prison for five months and fined 30,000 dollars. Many people would have fallen to their knees and pleaded innocent, but not Martha. While she always maintained her innocence, she went to jail without complaining and began knitting and crocheting for the other inmates. The knitted poncho Martha wore out of jail on her day of release was made by one of the other females sentenced to time in prison with her.

WALT DISNEY

Okay, one impossibility might be to find someone in North America (and most of the world) who doesn't know who Walt Disney is and the wondrous world he has created. According to Biography, he didn't step into success, in fact, his first animation studio in Kansas floundered and failed (Tate, 2012).

Walt Disney left for California and gained more success with Disney Bros. Studios, where he really made a name for himself– and a few of his closest friends, such as Mickey Mouse.

MALALA YOUSAFZAI

The most inspirational of all is Malala Yousafzai, born in Mingora, Pakistan in 1997. Malala said that she tells her story (*Malala's Story*, n.d.), not because it is unique, but because it is a common plight for many Pakistani women.

Her father ran an all-girls school in their village and Malala loved the opportunity she was given until the Taliban took over and banned many things, including girls getting an education at school. Malala began speaking out in Pakistan against the unfair treatment handed down by the Taliban. In 2012, she was shot in the left side of the head by a gunman who boarded the bus she was on. She woke up in a hospital in England and was told about all of the people who had heard of her story and wished her well.

After several surgeries and rehabilitation, she became known around the world as an advocate for women in Pakistan and was the youngest person ever to receive the Nobel laureate.

The first instinct of the four, now-famous people, above was not to curl themselves into a ball and admit defeat. They addressed their problems, made amends with the past, and propelled themselves toward success using mental toughness.

CHALLENGE YOURSELF: OVERCOME OBSTACLES

Sometimes, there are obstacles that you can not overcome, such as a chronic illness, being laid off, or having a spouse leave you. When you are left with something you cannot fix, you may feel lost, angry, and even depressed as a feeling of helplessness invades you.

When there are circumstances that you have no control over, focus on something that you can control to help you deal better with the loss or situation, such as:

1. Chronic illness: You may have lupus, diabetes, or fibromyalgia which makes you feel exhausted on a near-daily basis. This is something that can be managed through a doctor, but in large part, there is little that can be done to fight frequent bouts of extreme fatigue where you may find yourself in bed for most of the day. To maintain motivation, read a book series that gives you something to look forward to, or start writing a journal or that book you have always put off.

2. Made redundant at work: Rather than stay on the couch watching television all day, take an online course to upgrade your skills so that you can find a new, better job that you love.

3. Recently single: When someone decides they no longer want to be with you, it can be devastating. Rather than focus on what could have saved the relationship or why your partner stopped loving you, focus on the ones that love you and will always be by your side.

These exercises to promote mental strength and help you overcome obstacles can be challenging in the beginning, but if you keep at it, they will come as second nature, and soon you will be on the path to a new and exciting adventure and a refreshed view of how strong you can be.

KEY TAKEAWAYS

In this chapter, you learned that

- through difficult times, you should remember you are not alone.

- any obstacle can be overcome by someone who is willing to adapt to issues that arise rather than give in to them. Take away the power of an obstacle by identifying the issue, recognizing why you need to adjust your goals, and then use a different path to get to your desired destination.

- to avoid succumbing to obstacles, you must change how you perceive yourself, believe in your abilities, and set clear and attainable goals.

8

START WITH THE MOST DIFFICULT TASK

Prioritizing your tasks throughout the day will help you be more productive, and the most generative hours are over the first couple of hours of the day. Naturally, our productivity is highest in the peak hours of the morning when we are freshly awake and full of vigor as we enter our workplace or set up at home, so this is when the most difficult or important tasks should be performed. If we wait until later in the evening, our minds are not as sharp and our urgency is overcome by tiredness from making decisions and thinking all day. Completing difficult tasks early in the morning allows you to focus before the business of the day has truly begun.

Completing the most challenging and unpleasant task of the day first will also give you a feeling of accomplishment and, often, can make you feel as though there is nothing you cannot accomplish for the rest of the day (*Hardest or Easiest Work First? What the Research Shows*, n.d.).

Prioritizing the most difficult task early on may look something like:

- Someone looking for a new job may apply for three new jobs before leaving their house in the morning.

- A reporter may check in with the local news or police department before leaving for the office.

- A student may want to go over a chapter in their textbook before going to campus for their exam.

Knowing what needs to be done and carrying through with these good intentions are completely different. It's second nature for many people to pull out their phones and go on social media or watch videos rather than do something more productive. Carring through a difficult task will help you be more productive, remind yourself that it is your opportunity to get ahead in life, make a difference in the world, or get better grades.

Take a piece of paper and write down your most important reasons for doing what needs to be done. It may help you to visualize exactly what you are working so hard for and may help push you through those times you may feel like giving up.

For example, take a second job to save up the capital to open a new business so you can fulfill your dream of being your own boss and following your passion. Or you may have to earn extra money to help support your ailing parents in their time of need. You must write down reasons that are true to your specific situation. In most cases, your reasons may be painful, but don't let that stop you from being honest. I have found that pain has propelled me into making difficult choices that require intense mental strength.

WHY STARTING WITH THE MOST DIFFICULT TASK IS CRUCIAL

Starting with the most difficult task first thing in the day will not only get it out of the way but there are other reasons that we should do the most difficult task first. Mark Twain once said, "Eat a live frog first thing in the morning and nothing worse will happen to you the rest of the day." This refers to people completing the most unfavorable task they have for the day to get it done and then anything from then onward will be more pleasant.

There are some distinct advantages of getting the worst task done first thing in day, including:

1. Our energy is optimal first thing: More challenging tasks take more effort than simple ones; it's basic science. Our circadian rhythm, also known as our biological clock, runs according to our sleep schedule. We are most alert early in the morning, shortly after we wake up, and before we lose steam around mid-afternoon. Since we are more alert when we first wake, it makes sense to focus on more challenging

tasks that take the most energy and demand the most attention.

2. Helps Avoid Procrastination: Putting things off until later in the day, especially difficult tasks, is far too easy. By completing the challenging tasks in the morning, you are bypassing the chances of putting them off until you are too tired to complete them.

3. Ensures the Task is Completed on Time: Often, we underestimate how long something will take to complete. So, by starting the task early in the morning, we give ourselves enough time to finish it without running past the deadline. If we were to begin later in the day, we may run out of time to finish what we need to do.

4. Helps Motivate You to Complete Subsequent Tasks: If you have already knocked the most challenging task off your to-do list, then subsequent assignments will be easily completed.

5. Allows More Time for Important Tasks: You may find that as you begin your first task of the day that unexpected issues arise. You may need to do further research to complete a school paper, or perhaps you didn't have all the information you needed to apply for a new job. When you begin a challenging task early on in the day, there is more time for reaching out for help or getting extra information.

CHALLENGE YOURSELF EXERCISE: EAT THAT FROG

Using Mark Twain's method (Binder, 2018), choose the most difficult or unpleasant task that you have to do in a day and get it out of the way first. Some people say that they prefer completing a few easy tasks that take only a few minutes before diving into a more time-consuming task.

If you are having a difficult time diving into a hefty task first thing, begin with a few smaller chores that take no more than five minutes each. Once the easier assignments are complete, dive into the more challenging job. This way you will have a few items checked off your list and be more motivated to get to work on the more timely assignment at hand.

KEY TAKEAWAYS:

In this chapter, you learned that

- removing the most challenging task from your day first thing will set the momentum for the rest of the day.

- completing large tasks bits at a time can make them feel more manageable.

- doing the hardest task at the beginning of your day will give you a feeling of accomplishment, help avoid procrastination, and ensure the task is completed on time.

9

SUCCESSFUL PEOPLE ARE THOSE WHO ARE WILLING TO DELAY GRATIFICATION AND MAKE SACRIFICES IN THE SHORT TERM

Delayed gratification is almost unheard of in today's age of technological advances and era of instant gratification. Although most people thrive on instant gratification, delayed gratification and impulse control are essential life skills. It may not seem like it, but delayed gratification is the faster way to help realize your goals.

Despite what many people think, you can't get whatever you want as soon as you want it. Instant gratification is becoming a source of frustration because it creates an unreal sense of hope. Delayed gratification allows you to learn from mistakes and work up to what you deserve. But what exactly is delayed gratification?

Delayed gratification is one's ability to resist immediate gratification for an even deeper sense of gratification at a later time. Delayed gratification is correlated to impulse control. Those who have excellent impulse control exceed at waiting for delayed gratification, but this is also a skill that one can develop.

Children avoid disappointment and pain at all costs so they lack delayed gratification. As we age, we become more knowledgeable about the consequences that can be related to delaying gratification to avoid making a poor decision.

When we want something right away without putting in hard work, planning, or consideration, we deprive ourselves of building persistence. This can go back to children getting ribbons and accolades for literally nothing nowadays. All it does when you don't work hard for your accomplishments or wait to feel gratified is weaken your mind and give you a sense of entitlement.

7 TIPS FOR DELAYING GRATIFICATION

There are several ways to help ensure your success with delaying gratification (Cherry, 2020). The top seven ways are listed below.

1. Reward Yourself: Forming a habit is more likely to be successful when we are rewarded for our efforts, including by ourselves. Promise yourself that if you don't go shopping you will allow yourself to buy one new item on your next payday.

2. Practice Mindful Rest: Delayed gratification uses significant willpower and if you are going nonstop, you may find that you burn yourself out before you can complete your tasks. Taking a break to wind down mentally and reconnect with

nature or reading a book will go a long way to assure you have enough energy to complete your tasks.

3. Distract Yourself: You may want a piece of cake but you know that indulging will throw off your diet. Walk away from the temptation and go for a walk, read a book, or start going through your closet to get rid of unwanted items. Often, the distraction will remove the temptation entirely.

4. Is Giving in Worth it?: Imagine you are saving up to buy a house but continually become swayed to spend money on your love of new clothing. Think of the new home you so desperately want and consider if owning a new pair of shoes that will get dirty or buying a new purse that is just as functional as your old one is worth putting off your dream of being a homeowner.

5. Make a Budget: Purchasing items we don't need is one of the main forms of instant gratification. We want to feel happy and reward ourselves with new items.However, we often don't buy what we need, but what we want. Make a weekly budget and once you have reached your limit, stop. Having a budget can help prevent buying items you don't need.

6. Consider Your Merit: What are your core values? Do you need a new vehicle to make yourself happy just because your friend just bought one? Having shiny new things may make some people feel more important, but is that you?

7. Remember the Big Picture: Say you want to skip working out one day because you have better things to do or you think that missing one day won't hurt. While missing one day due to unforeseen circumstances can occur, putting off your health goals one day can lead to repetition. Remember the goal you set for yourself regarding weight loss, what you

are training for, or the health milestone you strive for, and ask yourself if it's worth it to put that off.

THE MARSHMALLOW EXPERIMENT

The Stanford marshmallow experiment (Zacharia & Parent, 2015) that was conducted by a psychologist named Walter Mischel in 1972, is an example of delayed gratification. The study was performed with children that were seated in a room with a tasty morsel of food, such as a marshmallow, and were told that if they were able to resist the treat, they would get an additional snack as opposed to eating the one treat right away.

Many children ate the treat as soon as the person conducting the experiment left the room, but other children resisted the temptation and reaped the rewards of an additional treat.

The results of the experiment showed that the children who resisted the initial offering and waited for the additional reward had many advantages over those children who did not demonstrate delayed gratification. The children that demonstrated restraint performed better academically and had elevated social skills, fewer substance abuse issues, and fewer behavioral issues.

Some additional examples of delayed gratification include:

- Career: Avoid going out late the night before a big presentation so you can feel well-rested and do a good job.

- Relationships: Rather than aggressively confronting your partner and engaging in an argument, you use communication skills to find a dignified resolution.

- Money: Resist making unnecessary, substantial purchases and instead save up your money for a larger purchase such as a car, vacation, or deposit on a house.

- Health: Resist the urge to eat something unhealthy and feel pleased with your decision later on and avoid a sugar crash.

EXERCISES FOR ENGAGING IN DELAYED GRATIFICATION

As with dieting and exercise, it is tempting to jump in all at once and deny yourself anything enjoyable to build up delayed gratification, but like anything, it pays to begin gradually. Do not deprive yourself of the small rewards that you have promised yourself after you have demonstrated delayed gratification.

Try the following steps to engage in delayed gratification for yourself:

- Begin Small: Perhaps you are trying to cut back on eating dessert because it has become a nightly habit. Rather than going cold turkey, try not eating dessert one night a week, then the next week skip dessert two nights, and so on until you are down to eating dessert once a week.

- Set Rules: Perhaps you have a habit of online shopping but then have buyer's remorse. Rather than purchasing something as soon as you see it, sleep on it. If you can't stop thinking about the purchase, then you should consider buying it. Another option might be to go into the actual store, when you can, to make sure you try the item on and genuinely like it.

- Be Grateful: Practice being grateful for all that you have to train your brain to thrive on delayed gratification. When you acknowledge all that you have, including new clothes, a car, and a home, you will realize that new items aren't necessary.

- Remember Why You're Doing It: When delayed gratification becomes difficult, remind yourself why you are doing it. If you are cutting back on spending, remember the house, the trip, or the car that you are saving for

We all want to be happy and believe that we are deserving of things that make us feel elated, but we often give into instant gratification for quick rewards rather than holding off for a much higher reward that comes with delayed gratification. To simplify, think of the children that passed up the opportunity to have two treats but took the singular treat for fear of missing out. Knowing about the marshmallow experiment now, you would likely hold off on eating the singular mallow. Why then would you cave to temptation knowing that something much greater was waiting for you just around the corner?

CHALLENGE YOURSELF EXERCISE: DELAY GRATIFICATION

Think of a big-picture item that you want. Are you saving for a trip, a new car, or perhaps you are saving for a wedding? Whatever you are squirreling money away for—most of us are saving for something–keep that image in the forefront of your mind. Whenever you go to spend money on something that you don't really need, consider if it is bringing you closer to your big-picture goal or if you are seeking instant gratification. If there is nothing to gain from the money being spent elsewhere, tuck it away in a jar, a drawer, or a separate bank account and you might be surprised to see how much-delayed gratification saved you.

KEY TAKEAWAYS:

In this chapter, you learned that:

- successful people use delayed gratification as a reward tool by resisting the temptation of an instant reward, knowing there will be a better reward if they wait.

- delayed gratification teaches us patience and the value of working hard now for a bigger opportunity down the road.

- there are daily ways to improve your delayed gratification skills through daily exercises such as delaying unhealthy actions, being optimistic, focusing on what you are able to do and accepting variability.

10

MOTIVATION AND MENTAL TOUGHNESS

Motivation can be fleeting, depending on our energy levels, our mood, what else is going on in our lives, and other fluctuating factors. What motivation boils down to is discipline, and like mental toughness, it is a learned trait.

When we learn self-discipline, we teach ourselves how to lead a more gratifying and productive life. With discipline comes the ability to make better decisions and create pathways that lead us to a more prosperous life mentally, physically, and emotionally. Discipline allows us to prioritize what is most important when reaching our goals and living a more fulfilling existence.

You may want to do everything at once when planning your future, but it needs to be taken step by step. When you focus on everything at once, you lose track of what you have done and what still needs to be completed. You wouldn't begin a meal by mashing the potatoes; they would be raw and hard. This also applies to building mental toughness. You won't be decisive and strong until you work out what you need to leave behind and work toward.

There are key strategies that can be implemented to strengthen self-discipline and create mental strength and powerful results in your personal and professional life.

DESIGNATE BLOCKS OF TIME

Set aside blocks of time each day or week to work on your goal, depending on what it is. If you are writing a book, set aside a 1-hour block of time each day to write, and little by little, you will be 28 hours into your book by the end of the month.

If you are clearing out a space in your home, carve out 15-minute increments of time each day to remove the first object of clutter that you see. This also works well with reorganizing and cleaning your home. When you walk into a room, tidy the first mess that draws your attention. At the end of the week, you will have spent nearly two hours tidying up or reorganizing.

REMOVE DISTRACTIONS

If you are trying to finish a report for school or work on a proposal for work but find yourself turning on Netflix or reaching for your phone, remove the distractions or remove yourself from the area where the distractions are.

Set up your workspace in a quiet area of your home that doesn't have a television and place any distracting items, such as your phone, well out of your reach or in another room. Rather than growing tired of your task at hand and reaching for the remote or going on social media, take a breath and redirect your focus to the task at hand. Gradually, your workspace will be a place where distractions are not even considered; it just takes time.

GIVE YOURSELF A BREAK

While chasing our dreams, we may make mistakes, such as cheating on a diet or abandoning our workout routine, but dwelling on this will do no good. Despite our best efforts, we have off days, and there is always a chance that life will throw a curveball that we need to dive in for. The important thing is that we forgive our indiscretions or lack of effort and move on. Tomorrow is another day.

EAT THE FROG

You know what this means! Procrastination is all too easy when a monumental task needs to be done. Rather than perplexing over it all day, dive into the worst or most demanding task that you have early in the day so that you can focus your prime energy on it and get it out of the way and make room for more pleasant or less frustrating tasks later on.

THE IMPORTANCE OF REPETITION IN DISCIPLINE

Repetition is crucial when we want to make significant improvements within ourselves or in our lives. Before you know what to repeat, you need to identify what it is that you want to change, improve, or strive for, and only then can you change the paradigm of what has been holding you back.

A paradigm is defined by Webster's Dictionary as, "Example, pattern. Especially: an outstandingly clear or typical example of the archetype."

A habit is formed by repeatedly and consistently doing something, such as biting your nails or eating junk food every night before bed. It may begin as something that you only did once or twice but as the weeks go on, it becomes more embedded in your subconscious and before you know it, you are down to your cuticles and pulling out chips from the pantry as part of your bedtime routine. Implementing good habits and reversing bad ones takes the same repetition and consistency.

If you want to eat healthier, you are going to change more than your eating habits and the foods you eat. You need to change the paradigm or pattern and habits that you are used to when it comes to eating. Changing a paradigm cannot be done with self-restraint alone, but there are two ways that you will be able to change it:

1. emotional impact

2. repetition

Emotional Impact refers to something that is so life-altering that you will never be the same. This is generally due to something negative occurring or, less frequently, something more positive occurring.

Repetition requires you to introduce yourself to something new. It is not necessary to have the information set to memory, but close your eyes and imagine the idea coming to fruition in your subconscious.

It is distinctly important to keep repeating these steps every day to disrupt the paradigm that is embedded in you. Once a pattern has ruled the roost for a long while, it has less desire to change than you can imagine. The little devil on your shoulder, called the paradigm, is going to urge you to skip your jogging day when you are heading to the closet to put on your running shoes. You will feel a strong urge to eat that cake when you know you should be reaching for the lettuce instead. There's always tomorrow to eat right and get fit, right? At least that's what the nagging voice wants you to believe.

This is where you need to begin to visualize a new picture over and over again until your subconscious holds onto it and can resist a resurgence of that nagging voice.

The initial image you put into your mind will be weak because it sits in your conscious mind, like a loosely planted flower. With repetitive imagery, the vision will become more deeply seeded in your mind and will become planted in the subconscious firmly.

As the image becomes more deeply embedded in your emotional mind, it becomes stronger and begins to override the previous image that is now weakening and becoming overturned. It is important that you become educated on what you are embedding in your mind because as it becomes deeply rooted, it will become the new subconscious that instinctively kicks in, even when you aren't thinking about it.

When you want to make a change in your life, it is crucial to change the paradigm. For example, if you want to be more consistent in your workout routine, think of yourself as an athlete. What do athletes do? They work out no matter what so they can keep up their rigorous training and hit their goal.

If you are trying to eat healthier, envision the foods that will nourish your body and how creative you can be with adding natural flavors. If you envision desserts as a way to deter yourself, you may actually be planting junk food into your subconscious, which will defeat the purpose.

REPETITION IS THE KEY TO LEARNING

All of us repeat several tasks daily, often without even thinking about it. We get up, brush our teeth, get dressed, make coffee, read the paper, check our phones, go to work, and many other things that just become second nature because we repeat them consistently.

To use repetition to improve discipline, you need to assign a part of every day to alter your paradigm. Every day, allocate some time to visualize in your mind what you want to do to make your life more fulfilling–to improve your mental strength. It doesn't have to be a great amount of time, even just 15-20 minutes each day will help set a new paradigm.

If you want to make your life something that you can be proud of, thrive in, and not merely exist in, spend time every day working toward your goals. Self-discipline needs to be initiated by you. No one else can get you to want something badly enough for you to sacrifice and work hard.

Some exercises to help you build self-discipline include:

1. Meditate: Meditation is one of the best forms of accomplishing self-discipline. Choose a block of time every day to connect to your inner self through meditation and delving into your thoughts. This form of relaxation and connecting with one's self is critical in forming a strong sense of self-discipline.

2. Make Your Bed Every Morning: Doing something as simple as making your bed every morning will help you strengthen your self-discipline. This small task will help start your day off with productivity and will help you feel that you have accomplished something, however small.

3. Morning Exercise: Begin each day with physical activity such as yoga, push-ups, a jog, or anything else that invigorates your body and kick-starts your mind.

4. Avoid Negative Outlets: Mentally tough people do not waste time with negativity. Negative people and outlets that serve as a source of pessimistic energy will only serve to induce self-pity and feelings of inadequacy. Mentally tough people

focus on the positive, what they can change, and avoid self-deprecating people and situations.

CHALLENGE YOURSELF: REPETITION IN EXERCISE

You can apply this to a number of activities (anything that can be repeated) but for this exercise, we are going with squats.

For the sake of preventing injury, follow these steps to perform a safe and proper squat:

1. Stand with your feet slightly wider than shoulder-width apart, straighten your back, lift your arms in front of you, and engage (tighten) your abdominal muscles.

2. With weight bearing on your heels, back straight, head held high, lower into a seated position until your body mimics how it would if you were sitting down.

3. Go back to a standing position.

4. Repeat.

The first time you do proper squats, you want to limit them to about five repetitions of 10 squats. This means that you will do 10 squats in a row then rest for about 20 to 30 seconds and then repeat. That may not seem like a lot, but for the beginning, it's a good amount. If you already do squats, perhaps add more reps or do the squats using dumbbells or kettlebells to add weight.

Repeat this challenge every day, increasing your numbers gradually by 5-10 each time. This repetition will make the squats easier to perform well and strengthen your muscles to do more over time. This type of repetition is key to learning a new skill well.

KEY TAKEAWAYS:

In this chapter, you learned that:

- motivation is the initial spark that sets your goals in motion. Do not forget that motivation is strongly correlated with self discipline.

- repetition and discipline are key to changing a paradigm. Rather than continuing to live in the past, or worrying about what is to come, live in the moment.

- repetition is the key to learning and setting a new positive habit, such as exercising every day, making your bed every morning, or avoiding unhealthy foods.

11

MENTAL TOUGHNESS AND THE UNITED STATES MILITARY

When you think of the United States military, you may assume that the largest, strongest, most intelligent cadets excel, but it is the ones who have mental toughness that finish first.

A member of the military needs to not only function under pressure, but they need to flourish, exceed expectations, and become stronger as they overcome obstacles. It is not muscular strength that will help cadets overcome what they face during training or on the front line, but the mental strength that comes with years of hard work and commitment.

The military is elite in igniting motivation in personnel and having individuals set goals that they work toward through discipline and mental toughness. Paratroopers, rangers, SEALs, and Green Berets need to go through rigorous training and self-discipline to show they are mentally strong. They exercise excessively, have a limited amount of food to eat, have sleep restrictions, and have several various stressors put on them to make sure they have the mental strength to carry on.

There is no doubt that anyone who steps up to be a member of the United States military has to be motivated to do so. No one joins believing that it will be a cake walk, but it is impossible to know how grueling it is without going through the training. This is what separates those who cannot from the mentally tough.

Those who join the military are driven by a love of their country and the willingness to protect their way of life. The training that goes into the cadets taps into their loyalty and willingness that they have to fight for what they believe in. Dedication is already a factor in most who join the military and mental toughness will follow with those who follow through on their training.

FOUR STEPS TO BUILDING MENTAL TOUGHNESS IN THE US MILITARY

Mental toughness is built gradually and needs to be done with persistent work and determination. Building resilience and mental toughness is a completely different thing in the military than it is for regular civilians.

When we eat that frog by completing our most hated task first thing in the day, such as going through emails, those in the military are eating a much, much more foul-tasting frog than the rest of us. Not even members of the military are mentally tough right out of the gate. They go through rigorous training to get to where they are physically and mentally.

Here are three steps that the military uses to improve mental toughness (Smith, n.d.):

1. Persistence: Once the initial excitement of a new venture has worn off, it is persistence that kicks in to keep you going toward your goal. Allowing your journey to take a back seat is going to weaken your stamina to cross the finish line. Propel yourself toward your objective every day and keep the momentum going.

2. Habit: We all have habits—some are good and some we need to train ourselves out of. It takes as much time to break a habit as it does to set one and both need daily effort and repetition. When you are setting a new habit, you must repeat the steps every day so that whatever you are trying to accomplish becomes second nature. Exercising every day is challenging at first, but after a few weeks, a habit is set and you feel less productive and lack energy if you don't exercise for a day. Eating healthy sets the same standards of well-being so your body needs healthy foods to keep it functioning optimally.

3. Discipline: The foundation of reaching your goals is discipline. When you lack motivation or energy, discipline is what keeps you going. Wallowing in self-pity will achieve nothing, but working toward your goals of exercising more, eating healthier, and meditating will help you move forward. You may know that you need to jog every day to train for a marathon but it's the discipline of getting up, lacing your shoes, and hitting the pavement that matters. Bruce Lee, the top martial arts expert the world ever knew, learned his craft through all of these steps. He practiced every day without fail and let nothing get in the way of his discipline and mental toughness.

CHALLENGE YOURSELF: GIVE IT YOUR ALL EVERY

DAY

This challenge is straightforward, but it takes determination. Take action toward building your dream every day. Don't let a single day go by that you don't work on some part of your plan that will lead you to your destination.

Taking a university course means opening your textbook every day and reading a chapter or making notes. Improving discipline means that you need to apply the initial steps to show up every day and give it everything you've got.

KEY TAKEAWAYS:

In this chapter, you learned that:

- the United States military is filled with mentally tough people, conditioned to withstand grueling tests.

- military toughness is built through conditioning, perseverance, determination, and habitual exercises.

- motivation is what it takes to sign up for the military, or any other physically and mentally demanding post, and perseverance is what keeps you in it when exhaustion kicks in.

12

HABITS OF MENTALLY TOUGH PEOPLE

Realizing your full potential does not mean that you need to take on more challenges and tasks than you already have on your plate. The smarter way to reach your goal is to, not work harder, but work smarter by removing unproductive tasks that can drain your energy and mental toughness.

Those who succeed in life do so by planning their time and their tasks carefully. A successful lawyer is not going to file the same deposition twice; it isn't necessary and it is a waste of time. So why would anyone add baggage to their lives, such as self-pity or fear of change, that will only hold them down.

Mentally tough people know how to delegate their time by prioritizing the most important commitments and tasks first. Below are seven additional habits that mentally tough people follow.

1. Embrace Change: By embracing change, you are inviting unlimited opportunities to come into your life by constantly adapting. If change is something that you dread, you will have a difficult time taking risks and engaging in growth.

2. Avoid Self-pity: The only thing that wallowing in self-pity is going to do is keep you stuck in the bad situation that you are in. Everyone goes through difficult times, whether it's losing a job, losing a partner, or having an illness. When we get lost in self-pity, we become fixated on the problem and are unable to see the solution.

3. Own your Circumstances: A victim mentality is a crutch for those who are mentally weak. They dissolve any power they have over circumstances and their own life and emotions by saying things like, My coworker makes me feel inadequate. You should never give anyone the power to control how you feel. Rather than giving others credit for your actions and emotions, use phrases like, I choose to get up early so I can get a head start on my work, rather than, I have to get to work early. Owning your circumstances and choices is a form of mental toughness.

4. Reserve Energy for What you Have Control Over: Energy spent worrying about what we cannot change is wasted energy. Rather than depleting your energy on what you cannot control, as unfortunate as the situation may be, focus instead on what you can control.

5. Don't Worry About Others' Opinions: There are always going to be those who want to bring you down and this has

nothing to do with you or what you stand for. In fact, it has everything to do with their own insecurities. Mentally tough people do not worry about what others think, nor do they make others feel inferior.

6. Embrace Failure: Now, this doesn't mean that you should purposely fail, but it does mean that you shouldn't be afraid to fail despite trying. When we are genuinely doing all that we can do to succeed, the failures we face along the way can only serve as reminders of what not to do in the future. If you are afraid to fail, you will never take risks that will inevitably lead to success.

7. Practice Emotional Intelligence: Mental toughness and emotional intelligence go hand in hand. You cannot move beyond frustrating times without the ability to deal with negative emotions and turn them into something more positive.

WHAT MENTALLY STRONG PEOPLE DON'T DO

Time and again, I have heard people declare how mentally strong they are. They insist they are advocates for self-worth and they don't need to answer to anyone because they are confident in their own abilities. These same people then post their lives on social media and thrive on the attention they receive regarding how they look, or what a good job they've done raising their kids or reorganizing their pantry.

Sharing your life with others is okay, but being fueled by comments, likes, and reposts is not going to make you feel any better about yourself if you are not already solidified in your feelings.

Now that you know the habits of mentally strong people, let's look at some of the things that mentally tough people will never do.

1. Spend Time with Negative People: We all know that someone who is constantly complaining about their lot in life, other people, or dwelling on some other bit of negative energy inevitably brings everyone down. We should surround ourselves with people and situations that make us feel good about ourselves and about life, not drag us into the recesses of negativity.

2. Give up on Themselves: Mentally tough people do not focus on monetary feelings, but on the goals they are working toward. They do not give up when they face hardships or when exhaustion kicks in. They are fueled by others' lack of belief in them and they will not let anything, not even failure, stand in the way of what they want.

3. Assume They Will be Disliked: Whenever a mentally weak person meets someone, they assume that they will not be liked. The negativity that engulfs them makes it difficult to believe that anyone could love, appreciate, or respect them enough to spend time with them.

4. Hold a Grudge: The emotional and physical damage of holding onto a grudge is more extensive than most account for. A grudge is saying that the negative individual or circumstance that thwarted you in some way is still in control of your emotions, validation, or success. Mentally strong people avoid stress and holding onto a grudge can cause an abundance of stress and result in high blood pressure and can lead to other detrimental emotional damages.

5. Count on Others for Happiness: Mentally strong people do not gauge their success or happiness on the accolades of others. If they feel good about what they have accomplished, they will not allow anyone to steal their good

vibes. On the other hand, if someone is super enthusiastic, they won't allow this to go to their head.

6. Do not Limit the Success of Others: Those who are truly mentally strong do not rely on the downfalls of others to help them feel good about what they have accomplished or to make themselves feel better when they are down. They know that comparing themselves to others isn't going to make them a better or worse person.

7. They are Void of Hope: Weak-minded people are often referred to as pessimists. They constantly believe that they are doomed for failure, and that good things happen only to other people and never to themselves. They are so stuck in a negative loop and they whine about their disadvantages in life but never do anything to help boost their odds.

BUILD RESILIENCE IN MENTAL STRENGTH

Whether it be from a person or on the news, a mentally strong person doesn't let negative people or things limit their outlook. Fixating on the state of a failing economy or investing every waking hour in a war overseas that cannot be controlled by our government, let alone an ordinary citizen, is a waste of our emotional resources. A mentally tough person avoids giving energy to what they cannot change.

Below are some exercises to help turn stress into resilience:

MAKE ANXIETY WORK FOR YOU

Our minds are fascinating things. According to Simply Psychology, depending on how we manipulate the brain's plasticity, we can be either an anxious wreck or we can teach it to reassess a circumstance and reframe our mental state to make more beneficial decisions.

By reminding ourselves that all emotions, even anxiety, have a place in propelling us to a better place, we can motivate ourselves to move forward. For example:

- Fear, if we allow it to, can trigger a negative response that paralyzes our ability to focus on anything else and eliminates our accessibility to change. Or, fear can encourage us to take a pause and reflect on why things didn't work out for us before and allow us to create an alternate direction that leads to opportunities.

- Anger is a powerful emotion and can debilitate your potential. It can also heighten your attention and remind you what your values and goals are.

- Worrying about things can lead to procrastination as you may want to prolong the perceived inevitable rather than dive in. If we embrace our worrying thoughts, we can adjust expectations and set a goal that is more attainable and realistic.

- Frustration can stunt your potential or make you quit before you complete a task. Instead, use it to challenge yourself to find a way to move around the challenge despite the struggle.

- Sadness is something that we all experience in our lives, but it's how we deal with it that matters. We can let this emotion steal our motivation or we can use it to reimagine our lives and goals to change our circumstances for the better.

VISUALIZE SUCCESS

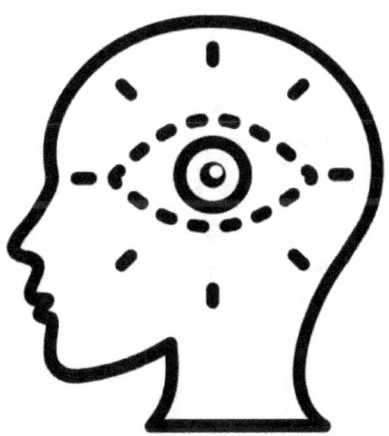

It's human nature to worry about things such as whether we did a good enough job at work, if we passed our test, or if our children are going to be happy. What you can do to build mental strength is to rephrase those thoughts to visualize an outstanding scenario for all of those questions. Your children are happy and loved and successful. Your job loves you and you will get that raise or promotion, and the test that you're worried about? You aced it!

You may think that setting your hope so high is a recipe for disaster, but it actually helps build the expectation that you have for yourself and your life, which allows you to go for what you want unapologetically and with gusto.

3. Get Outside

Getting out in nature is one of the best things you can do for a mental reset and to gain mental clarity. Not only will you get much-needed fresh air, but the distractions at the beach, park, or anywhere you enjoy being, are just wildlife and organic scenery. Giving yourself the opportunity to get outside every day will help make space for your thoughts, even if they are only quietly telling you to relax.

CHALLENGE YOURSELF: VISUALIZE YOUR BEST LIFE

At the beginning or end of every day, envision what your absolute best life looks like. Envision your house, those you love, your job, and where you live. How do you feel about yourself and the decisions you have made today that will move you closer to your best life? Work on altering your decisions and thoughts to envision what you want the story of your life to look like as the book closes.

KEY TAKEAWAYS

In this chapter, you learned that

- mentally tough people share a commonality in their determination to adapt, such as they don't worry about what others think, avoid self-pity, and embrace change.

- mentally strong people do not give up on themselves, spend time with negative people, or hold grudges.

- you can turn stress into resilience by embracing fear as a chance to reflect on what you can change, or use frustration as a challenge to find a way around the problem despite the struggle.

13

THE ABILITY TO FOCUS AND VISUALIZE YOUR GOALS

Consider your favorite athlete mounting the pitch, taking to the ice, or getting ready to compete in the CrossFit games. Now, do you think they are considering how they can mess up or how so many variables could shift beyond their favor? Of course not. Instead, they are focusing on the outcome that they want, whether it's hitting a home run, defending their goalie, or hitting their rep max.

Could you imagine your favorite team telling each other they were feeling a loss coming on or weren't sure if they were going to play well at all? Obviously, you wouldn't be rooting for that team. You want to cheer for the ones that visualize a win and have the mental strength to pull it off.

People who want to do well focus on the positive outcome and have no room for the negative. Just as we should not have a plan B lest we will use our valuable energy resources on thinking up a secondary plan, we need to envision the best-case scenario with everything we do.

We accomplish what we believe we are capable of. When we see ourselves failing at writing our first novel or we don't believe we can run a mile without breaking from exhaustion, we bring those visions to reality. Challenge the way you see the outcome by visualizing the steps you need to take to accomplish those goals gradually. Nothing worth having comes all at once, but we do need to envision the big picture.

In the last chapter, I listed visualizing success as a way to build resilience as strength, and the same applies here. When you focus on what you want and visualize your intended goal, your chances of success are greater than if you imagine failure.

WHAT EXACTLY IS VISUALIZATION?

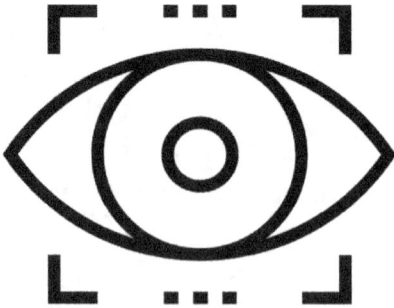

Visualization is a common technique that can be used to help you focus on some event that is important to you. When you have practiced visualization every day, you will help determine the outcome of the speech you will give, the test you are taking, or the marathon you are about to run. Visualizing the intended outcome will help you grow more confident in your abilities and it can promote a more favorable outcome.

Some people think that by considering all negative scenarios they are running out the bad ideas and bad luck, so to speak, so that all that is left is success. We now know that isn't the case and the negativity that circulates through your mind before you go for a job interview or go on a first date can harm the experience.

Running with the idea of the first date, instead of thinking about all that can go wrong—such as losing a button on your dress shirt, spilling water across the table, or running out of things to say—consider all that can go right. Imagine having a wonderful time, being funny, and finding humor in anything that does go awkwardly wrong.

Visualization can make you more eager for what you want. For example, your dream is to move to Los Angeles, so how can you use visualization to increase your yearning to move to the City of Lights. You begin to watch 4K videos on YouTube, or flip through TikTok or Instagram at influencers that post local pictures. Having these visuals will help your goal of moving to LA in your conscious and subconscious mind.

There are many benefits to using visualization techniques, such as:

- Increasing confidence and believing that you are able to achieve all that you visualize for yourself.

- Visualization is a technique that anyone can use, regardless of who they are or what they have and it doesn't take any special skill, just practice.

- When you visualize the path you will take to succeed in life or love, including all you need to do to get there, you will realize those steps leading you to where you want to go in reality.

ACHIEVING YOUR GOALS THROUGH VISUALIZATION

Visualization is something you can use to promote success in every aspect of your life. From opening your own business to making new friends, visualization will help you prepare for and help execute these plans. According to a study in the National Library of Medicine, many highly successful and effective individuals use visualization unwaveringly to help achieve their goals.

Our minds are extremely powerful and, with focus, can help us not only believe that we can accomplish certain things, but can help give us the perseverance to get them done. The ability of our mind is only limited to what we are able to visualize.

Beginning your own visualization journey is simple using the following steps:

1. Choose a Goal: The first step of achieving your goals through visualization is to know what you want. Choose one thing to focus on and begin visualizing how you will get what you want. Visualize the job you want, your health goal, or any one thing you are passionate about and that is what you are going to focus on. You may have several goals and dreams but visualize one at a time or you will not have a clear pathway to success.

2. Visualize Exactly What You Want: Picture exactly the scenario you want to occur. Focus on every single detail in your mind, leaving everything to your imagination and holding it there in your mind's eye. The more detail you can

muster, the more likely success will follow. When you picture the scene in your vision, what are the colors that you see? What do you smell? Is it cold, warm, or hot in temperature? Use all of your senses to bring to life what you are visualizing so it feels like your thoughts surround you.

3. Visualize Each Step of Your Journey: Let's say you are training for a triathlon. Picture every step, from the starting line as you dive into the ocean to begin your swimming portion of the race. Who is standing on the shoreline cheering you on? Imagine the people clapping as you come out of the water and get ready for the cycling portion of the triathlon. What is the weather like? How do your legs feel as you transition from the water to a bike? Imagine dismounting the bike and taking off your helmet as you begin the last, running portion of the race. Visualize the rush you feel and how you can keep going on forever. Imagine the finish line and the crowd cheering as you come across the line victoriously.

4. Visualize Your Goal Daily: If your triathlon is one month away, take time out of every day to visualize the entire triathlon to completion and continue up until the day of the triathlon. This doesn't mean that you need to go through the entire 3-hour race, but run a cliff note version of the key milestones including great detail. Running through the triathlon each day will train your mind to visualize success and bring it to fruition. Visualize your swim stroke, the road you are cycling along, how you will handle the hills, and the speed and technique you will use for the final running leg of the journey.

5. Visualize this journey while you are driving, jogging, or anytime during the day that you have time to focus completely on this technique to better train your mind to expect success.

VISUALIZATION TECHNIQUES

Visualization is a technique that helps bring dreams to reality by training your mind to believe that what you are envisioning will become reality. A mind is a powerful tool that is malleable and can promote success through habitual thinking.

Below are some tips to help optimize your visualization techniques:

- Choose a Quiet Place: For visualization techniques to be fully effective, you will need to do them in a quiet place and without distractions. It takes away from the exercise if you need to regroup or refocus your visualization with every interruption.

- Use an Image to Induce Visualization: If you are saving money to go to Scotland, it might help to keep a photo of Edinburgh Castle near where you do your visualizing. This way you will have a head start in the emotional and mental picture you want to paint for yourself.

- Write Your Goal as if it is a Mantra: Writing a short sentence that represents what you want to visualize will help keep the goal in mind. For example, if you are trying to change your diet to promote health, you could write, "I will eat healthier to be healthier."

Making headway toward your dreams is difficult if you don't use visualization to see clearly what it is you are striving for. Take time each day to focus on your goals and see them clearly in actuality.

CHALLENGE YOURSELF: MAKE A MAP OF YOUR FUTURE SUCCESS

A fun visualization come-to-life technique you can use is making a success map. This map should have a detailed list (in map form) of all things you need to do to make it to your ultimate goal. This map will lead you straight to realizing your goals.

KEY TAKEAWAYS

In this chapter, you learned that

- top athletes focus on the outcome they want to see at the end of a game or race, not what they are afraid might go wrong. We accomplish what we believe we are capable of.

- achieving your goals through visualization is a powerful tool. Visualization techniques allow you to see, taste, smell, and feel exactly what you want your outcome to be. When you focus on what you want and visualize your intended goal, your chances of success are greater than if you imagine failure.

- your mind is a powerful tool that is malleable and can facilitate success through implementing positive habits. When using visualization techniques, choose a quiet place, use a detailed image to set a scene, and repeat your goal as though it were a mantra.

14

MENTALLY TOUGH PEOPLE NEVER QUIT

Those who are truly mentally tough never quit. They learn from previous mistakes and then make things happen. The common theme throughout this book is that mental toughness can be learned and that it is a common trait among those who have led a challenging life.

We are not born with mental toughness but the circumstances that we face in life ignite a fight or flight mode and we can either collapse under the pressure of adversity or overcome them and allow them to strengthen us through the lessons they teach.

Just as mistakes can help us become more successful, trying times help make us stronger. You could say that building mental strength is similar to Charles Darwin's theories of survival of the fittest and natural selection. Those who are willing and able to adapt will survive and thrive.

Being mentally tough doesn't mean that you have to imagine a monumental accomplishment for yourself, it means that you need to dive into everything you do with persistence and honor. Many people who are mentally strong fight through obstacles with the goal of surviving, only to realize that, once they are through to the other side, they have an abundance of knowledge to share with others.

Some people choose to be mentally tough to accomplish their goals, but others are thrust into a life or position that they never asked to be in and have to find strength just to survive. Children never ask to be put into situations that require them to build mental toughness before they even know what it means, but the harsh reality is that sometimes it happens.

The world is full of mentally tough people from all backgrounds who go on to lead extraordinary lives, but being mentally strong doesn't mean you need to live your life in a large way. Some of the strongest people chose to live a quiet life, while others thrive in the spotlight or use a larger platform to promote positivity and live life to the fullest despite hardships.

Some of these notable people include:

- Charlize Theron: To most, Charlize Theron is an actress born in South Africa that is known for her roles in movies such as Monster, Mad Max: Fury Road, and Atomic Blonde. What you may not know, according to multiple outlets including Biography, is that the actress had a volatile childhood with a father that was an alcoholic and beat Charlize and her mom frequently and made threats against their lives. One day, when Charlize was only 15 years old, her mother killed her father during a fight ("Charlize," 2019).

- Charlize's mother was found not guilty due to self-defense and continued to raise her daughter. Charlize struggled through school, didn't fit in, and had chronic health issues. Eventually, the actress found her calling in acting and although she doesn't speak much on the topic of her upbringing, she is a true example of someone who rises out of a terrible situation and becomes mentally strong enough to realize their dreams.

- Stephen King: This world-renowned author is known as the King of Horror but he grew up extremely poor, raised by a single mom who struggled to make ends meet, and faced countless rejections well into his adult years. King, who was rejected by countless literary agents, tossed his first number one bestseller, Carrie, into the garbage because he was convinced it would be discarded like all his other novels. His wife dug Carrie out of the trash and convinced him to send it to agents.

- It was only through decades of perseverance that Stephen found his niche in the darkness of horror writing and millions of fans that crave his twisted, dark tales. If not for mental strength and determination, none of us would have classics like Misery, The Shining, or The Green Mile.

- Keanu Reeves: There are few Hollywood actors as beloved as Keanu Reeves. His films, such as the Matrix, have captivated generations, but it is his backstory that makes him mentally strong. Keanu grew up in Lebanon, raised by a single mother after his father left when he was only three years old. His mother remarried four times and Keanu moved around often as a child. Keanu had to find mental strength that many cannot when his 8-month-old baby died, followed by the love of his life. He also helped nurture his sister for years as she battled cancer. Through all of these challenging times, he remained strong and resilient, donating to charities and being a pillar of strength for those lucky enough to be in his circle of friends and family.

- Bethany Hamilton: While surfing in the waters of Hawaii, Bethany Hamilton found herself fighting for her life at only 13-years-old. A shark bit off her left arm and she nearly bled to death. Rather than let this horrendous attack deter her from her dreams, Bethany was back on her surfboard one month later and continued to practice what she loved. Just two years later, at age 15, Bethany competed in the Explorer Women's Division of the NSSA National Championships and won first place. The incredible courage and mental toughness that it took for Bethany to get back in the water is outstanding. She had to accept that a shark took her arm and she had to adapt and persevere with only one arm, but she wasn't about to let it steal her dreams.

NEUROSCIENCE BEHIND PERSEVERANCE

Perseverance is what differentiates those who win and those who quit. What is it that kicks in during difficult times that separates those who can and those who won't? In part, we can put it down to dopamine–a chemical in the body that helps you feel motivation, enthusiasm, excitement, and accomplishment ("The Neuroscience," n.d.).

Dopamine keeps us motivated and working on achieving our goals. Dopamine can be increased through habitually challenging and changing your behavior. According to Psychology Today, researchers have linked increased dopamine levels to forming habits such as perseverance.

Neuroscientists have done research to determine the link between dopamine and the reinforcement of good behavior and perseverance and good habits.

Dopamine and the link it has to propel one to their goals is not new to neuroscientists, but what has been recently found is that dopamine directly correlates with good and bad habits. This was found in a study that determined key receptors for the production of dopamine acted like a pathway to the formation of habit-forming behavior.

Research done in the field of neuroscientific research shows that significant levels of dopamine might be the differential between someone who perseveres and someone who is more likely to give up. While dopamine is not the only propelling factor in perseverance, it has a significant impact.

We all like rewards. The dopamine reward system works through an intricate structure throughout the brain. This system gives us a feeling of happiness, contentment, or excitement after such things as eating, resting, or being with friends. Dopamine travels through your brain and gives you a feeling of satisfaction as a reward for something that you have done, thereby making it something that you want to continue working on.

This system is used as a warning of types in the animal kingdom. Animals seek out what makes them feel good as a way to avoid pain. The animals in nature seek the greatest reward and, in turn, are rewarded by affirmation in a sense of security. As humans, we seek different rewards than a lion would, but it is all on the same spectrum of how we respond to a task or incident in hopes of a return of gratification.

PERSEVERANCE MEANS NO SAFETY NET

There has never been a successful person who had a back-up, or back-out plan, as it should be referred to. Once you have determined your goal, visualized it, and gotten to work making it a reality, there should not be a plan B that gives you an easy out to abandon your goal in lieu of something easier. Perseverance means that you determine your goals and you stick to those goals, dodging obstacles and climbing over roadblocks to get to where you need to be. Having a plan B to fall back on can lower your chances of success significantly.

Historically, the great commanders during times of war would burn bridges they had just crossed or ships that they rode to arrive at their destination as a way to cement their commitment to moving forward; retreat was not an option. This show of determination was to be an example to their troops and to show their resolve and that what they were fighting for was worth battling to the end.

A similar *die-on-your-sword* tactic can be applied by those securing a business loan. An entrepreneur may put up their house as collateral as a show of good faith that they will not default on their loan. This shows the bank, or other lending agents, that they are planning for success. This is also an initiative for the business owner to put in their best effort not to let their business endeavor fail.

There are contingencies that can be kept in place while you are building your dreams that wouldn't constitute a plan B. For example, if you are starting your own business but have a freelancing job that is paying the bills until the main event takes over, that isn't considered you having a secondary plan in case you fail. It's called paying the bills while working hard to achieve your dreams.

Let's say you want to open a cafe with a bookstore attached in the downtown core of your city, only when you get through the business plan and put everything in place to look for a building, there is already one there. This may mean you have to rethink your location or the coffee shop and bookstore combination. Having the foresight to recognize that things can change shows forethought and adapting to that change demonstrates mental toughness. When we are ready for the unexpected, we are less likely to make decisions while emotions run high.

Mental strength means delving into your inner core and persevering despite all the setbacks and naysayers. Our brains are wired to respond to positive interactions and habits, making repetitive good actions something that we begin to automatically achieve.

And as with all who have paved the way to success before you, failure is not an option when you have perseverance. When things are difficult, push onward, burning that bridge so there is no going back. A contingency plan means safety, not failure, as long as it carries you toward your initial goal and doesn't sidetrack you to a plan B.

CHALLENGE YOURSELF: DAILY VISUALIZATION FOR PERSEVERANCE

It's easy to give up on your dreams and to allow perseverance to fall. But you're here because you want to build mental strength and succeed at your goals, so challenge yourself to maintain the drive to succeed by engaging in these exercises.

ALTER YOUR PERCEPTION

The only thing that is keeping you from reaching your goals is the belief you have in yourself. Change the perception that you have of your abilities and the chances that you will succeed. You will only reach your goals if you toss statistics and probabilities out the window. This is on you and you are capable of succeeding.

TURN CHALLENGES INTO OPPORTUNITIES

Perspective is the main challenge in reaching your goals. While one person sees failure as the end game, another will see it as a way to learn and grow. By viewing challenges as opportunities, there is nothing that can stand in your way of success.

MAKE IT ABOUT YOU

When you envision your goals, you need to see yourself in them. If you want to be wealthy and choose a career based on that alone, chances are you will lose focus and motivation pretty quickly. But when you see your future and passion in your dreams, you are more likely to persevere. Envision yourself in your goals daily, making it all about you and your success.

KEY TAKEAWAYS

In this chapter, you learned that

- there is strength in addressing and learning from your mistakes. If you procrastinate about finishing a file for work and hand it in late, next time work on it a bit every day to avoid not completing it on time.

- perseverance is the difference between someone who moves forward through difficulty and someone who quits.

- setting up a plan B gives you an excuse to quit; don't do it.

15

MENTALLY TOUGH PEOPLE DON'T SPEND TIME WITH WEAK, UNDISCIPLINED PEOPLE

Remember when your parents encouraged you to play with everyone at school and not flock to the pretty or popular girl, or the boy that had everyone swooning because he was the jock? While many people will be drawn to *shiny* people, those who seem to have the most curb appeal, you should surround yourself with those that represent who you want to be.

You can look at it as almost a mob mentality, but on a smaller scale. When you think of a teenager with four of his friends trying to get school work done while the other four want to go play video games instead of study, chances are he will go with them and abandon his studies. Now if the roles were reversed and there was one person who wanted to go play video games and four that wanted to study, chances are the one would forgo the games to work with their friends. This is what the sum of five speaks to; a self-help book by Paula Owens. The tendency of people is to go with the majority.

There is a saying that we are the sum of the five people that we spend the most time with. Keeping that in mind, have you surrounded yourself with people of substance, drive, compassion, and mental strength? Or have you gathered a posse of people that make you feel better about yourself because they haven't got their lives together or count on you for external validation?

Everyone you are in a relationship with—from romantic and platonic relationships to those you do business with—should be someone you admire and respect, someone that supports your dreams but has aspirations of their own. There is a reason that you choose to spend the majority of your time with your inner circle, even if it is on a subconscious level.

Self-stimulation: Our minds are like a muscle that grows with the wealth of knowledge it receives. We learn more through our environment, and that includes who we spend the majority of our time with. Seek out people who help challenge your thinking and with whom you can engage in thought-provoking conversations.

Quips and quarrels over political views, world news, and other stimulating conversations are not something to shy away from, but something to encourage. Sitting in a room full of people whose interests are in the Netflix catalog are not going to help you grow as an intellectual.

Healthier Habits: Consider what the outcome would be if you spent your time around people with no motivation or drive to better themselves. You would likely be unmotivated and stuck in a rut that provided mediocrity. The same can be said for being around physically active people who take care of their bodies and minds. Those around us have a significant impact on our habits, including the good, so if you want to become a more health-conscious person, the likelihood of success being around others who eat pizza and soda every day is pretty slim.

If four out of five friends are health conscientious, the probability of the fifth falling in line is much greater than the other four beginning to be careless with their workout routine. If you need the motivation to implement healthier habits, surround yourself with people who will be a good influence.

Greater Self-Esteem: When you surround yourself with people who are always striving to do and be better and encouraging you on your own journey, a deeper sense of community emerges. You don't need anyone to tell you your dream is worthwhile, but having people that believe in you, cheering you along, will give you a greater sense of confidence.

SHOW ME YOUR FRIENDS AND I'LL SHOW YOU YOUR FUTURE

Daniel Stephen Pena, Sr, who is credited with birthing the phrase "Show me your friend and I'll show you your future," is an

American philanthropist, businessman, and business coach. His philosophy with this phrase is that people take on the traits of those they most commonly attach themselves to, whether it is family, friends, or coworkers. We adapt to the traits and habits of those around us most.

Many adults don't believe they could be swayed into being like their friends. They believe they have a mind of their own, but it's not entirely true. How many times have you heard someone say that they need to stop hanging out with a certain friend because all they ever do is drink when they are around them? Have you heard someone complaining that they haven't gone to the gym because their brother would rather watch television and go to the movies together?

Just as negative habits and traits that others possess can pass onto us, so can positive attributes. You are a product of those around you and you will become like them so choose wisely who you spend time with. Dissecting who you spend the most time with and how they impact your life is not easy, but if you are determined to live the life that you have chosen for yourself, take accountability for your future and the people who will help shape it.

We don't make friends for temporary measures; we connect with people we enjoy spending time with and who we expect to have meaningful relationships with for decades to come. When you consider those you spend the most time with now, do they hold the same core values as you do? They don't have to be identical, but do they care about others and friendship, and want to succeed in life?

If you get annoyed with the immature antics of your friends now, can you imagine how pathetic the same attitude is going to be in 20 years? People can change and grow, but when you see no growth in your top five friends, it's time to think about cutting ties with them.

There are seven traits of resilient relationships, according to Psychology Today. They are:

1. Active Optimism: Rather than simply hoping things go well, active optimism is believing that there will be a good outcome and taking steps to lead to that outcome. In any type of relationship, this means that you both agree not to say critical or hurtful comments that can lead to arguments and negative consequences.

2. Decisiveness: This is knowing what you want and being strong enough to take the steps to get there. Decisive action leads to mental strength, such as when someone leaves a toxic work environment.

3. Tenacity: This is persevering when you are faced with failure, adversity, or discouragement. This can apply to the relationship you have with your friends, parents, and children—or it can mean fighting for a career or dream.

4. Integrity and Responsibility: Relationships that are built on loyalty and all parties acting with integrity and respect, are likely to be more resilient. This means being completely honest no matter the outcome and then working together to reach a common ground.

5. Self-Control: In relationships, resisting temptation, using impulse control, and using delayed gratification are critical for success. When we practice self-control, we avoid actions that will impact the relationship in a negative way and help implement healthy coping mechanisms.

6. Honest Communication through Connectedness: In a relationship, the feeling that you belong is built through

honest communication. This type of communication can help you feel connected to the person, even when the conversation is less than pleasant.

7. Present-Mindedness: When you are present of mind, you are opening pathways for more meaningful interactions within your relationship. This can lead to open communication and working together in collaboration for something better.

MENTALLY TOUGH PEOPLE ALIGN WITH LIKE-MINDED PEOPLE

Mentally tough people align themselves with those who have similar values. They do not allow weak-minded individuals to waste their time or give them the opportunity to bring them down.

Strength is built with perseverance and a firm understanding of your core values, which let the world know who you are and what you stand for. Likewise, if someone decides you are not worth their time, don't waste your energy trying to convince them otherwise.

Exercises to Discover Your Core Values

Fulfillment is gained by living life according to your core values. Personal fulfillment is determined by defining your core values, which will lead you to follow a path in life you believe in and help you make decisions based on what is important to you.

For this exercise, all you will need is a sheet of paper and a writing tool. Next, write down the three paramount things in your life, such as:

- achievement
- accountability
- health
- family
- intelligence
- compassion
- calmness
- balance
- success
- wisdom

If there are other core values that mean more to you, feel free to use those.

Once you have your top three core values, incorporate them into activities that you perform every day. If health is one of the three core values that mean the most to you, then you would make choices each day that promote optimal health, such as eating healthy, meditating, and exercising.

This exercise helps you find joy in everyday life and encourages you to create it yourself. Your life should consist of your core

337

values, including friends that help make you who you are.

It isn't always clear who is going to help keep you on the path to living a successful and fulfilling life versus those who will steal your spirit and drag you down with self-pity. Just because someone is mentally weak doesn't mean they are a bad person, but they could be unknowingly putting you at risk of sliding into the same rut.

Those who are mentally weak often:

1. Dwell on the past: Mentally weak people have a tendency to stay in the past and dwell on mistakes of themselves or of others. As I've mentioned, there is no moving forward in life and out of a negative state if you have one foot in the past. Instead of revisiting what went wrong with their relationship, job, or whatever else ails them, they are steadfast in repeating the same narrative.

2. Trust others too easily: Trust is not a bad virtue, but when someone immediately trusts people in their life, or even strangers, a host of adverse situations can arise. Trust should be earned by everyone, not given simply because they are someone you happen to know. Anyone can put up a facade about their happy life and moral values initially, but it's how those same people act behind closed doors that will define their core values. Someone who is overly trusting can be easily influenced by others with ill intent and can even be coerced into dangerous situations by shady people. Those who are mentally weak have the views and opinions of others easily impressed on their minds.

3. Over-analyze situations and people: Not everything needs to be analyzed. There are aspects of one's life that should have careful forethought–such as buying a house, choosing a partner, deciding to have children, and other life-altering events–but not everything needs to have so much thought put into it. Analytical thinking is detrimental because it

keeps us stuck in the past, in a place that we regret with decisions we wish we never made. When someone overthinks what they could have done differently or puts too much forethought into an event coming up, they are wasting time on something that literally cannot be changed. Take the time to think about the right decisions, analyze monumental life moments, and take action to do it right in the future or not at all.

4. Engage in self-pity: Self-pity is a key trait in someone that is weak-minded. It's okay to feel let down by something not going your way, but feeling sorry for yourself is not an inevitable response—it's a direct choice. Self-pity is a loop of constant betrayal of oneself. There is nothing good that can come from it because, much like over-analyzing, self-pity is consuming and it becomes easier to revel in the pity of others who may give you attention for your troubles.

5. Become envious of others: Mentally weak people have a tendency to envy what others have, whether it's money, a career, children, or their spouse. They don't put in the necessary effort to improve their opportunities, yet they still wish they had what belongs to someone else.

6. Hold onto anger: There is no point in holding on to anger and refusing to forgive or move on from a negative experience. Holding onto anger has a negative response from the brain and can lead to depression, cause sleep issues, and manifest into physical ailments. Being angry with someone is not something a mentally tough person would do; they would move on and use the experience as fuel to move on. A person who is mentally weak will dwell on and perpetuate the negativity in their everyday lives.

7. Spend time with mentally weak people: Are You Spending Time With the Right People? Are your top five people worth

your time? Keeping the principle that we are a compilation of the five people we spend the most time with, do your top five people represent examples of who you want to be in life? You can go so far as to make a list of the people you see most and what you admire about them compared to what you don't necessarily respect.

You may notice the pros outweigh the cons and stand by your current crowd, or you might realize that those closest to you don't have your back or follow the same ethical path you do and it might be time to make some changes.

KEY TAKEAWAYS

In this chapter, you learned that:

- mentally tough people don't spend time with weak, undisciplined people. Mentally tough people align with like-minded people.

- resilient relationships, such as those between mentally tough people, are supportive, honest, decisive, and respectful of one another's boundaries.

- the five people you spend the most time with influence your decisions.

CONCLUSION

Resilience is the keystone of mental strength. It is the difference between someone who bounces back from adversity and someone who is swallowed by defeat.

Do you want to be someone who wades through ambitions but never dives in, or do you want to do more than tread water with your life? There is staying afloat in this world and allowing others to dictate what we can or cannot accomplish or handle, and then there is you telling everyone that you've got your own back and will be all that you please.

Circumstances may throw a wrench in your plans. Use that detour to strengthen your resolve and learn how to put a contingency plan in place so you are not stalled in your future progress. No one is going to become their strongest mentally without having a few setbacks, but you need to look back at your missteps and avoid taking that same path again.

Having mental strength is believing in yourself and the road you have laid ahead of you. Living your best life isn't easy, but remember to choose your hard. Do you want a hard life of constant struggle and disappointment or do you want to work hard to get ahead?

Perseverance and determination are the cornerstones of all mentally tough people. There is no one, regardless of status in life or the advantages they have had, that is given strength. It is more often that those who have struggled greatly and come through challenging circumstances have the power of mental toughness.

BREAKING DOWN MENTAL TOUGHNESS

The power of mental toughness is in you; you just need to unleash your potential. We are not born with mental toughness, but we are born with the ability to learn resilience, determination, and discipline.

Make sure you are steadfast in your goal of empowering yourself with mental toughness by remembering to

- acknowledge your feelings

- focus on health

- externalize your feelings

- work toward goals each day

- assess your challenges

- practice self-compassion

- practice mindfulness

- project how you want to be treated

- choose your company wisely

- eat that frog

We alone are capable of building mental toughness. With every step we take and the boundaries we set, we build our mental strength and embrace the life we deserve.

GET YOUR POWER

The fact that you want to change is already the first step to making a huge difference in the strength you exude and are building.

While others complain about the challenges they face or vocalize their disdain for their lot in life, you are turning your opposition into opportunities and visualizing the life you want, despite the obstacles you may face now.

It doesn't matter where you are in your life; mental strength can be developed and strengthened at any time. Highlight the key points that resonated with you throughout this book and set into motion the plan that you have for using the power of mental toughness.

REFERENCES

6 strategies for overcoming obstacles that hold you back from success. (2020, August 5). Life Hack. https://www.lifehack.org/880737/overcoming-obstacles

7 characteristics of resilient relationships . (n.d.). Psychology Today. https://www.psychologytoday.com/gb/blog/when-disaster-strikes-inside-disaster-psychology/201804/7-characteristics-resilient

Buchecker, M., & Degenhardt, B. (2015). The effects of urban inhabitants' nearby outdoor recreation on their well-being and their psychological resilience. *Journal of Outdoor Recreation and Tourism, 10,* 55–62. https://doi.org/10.1016/j.jort.2015.06.007

Charlize Theron. (2019, October 9). Biography. https://www.biography.com/actors/charlize-theron

Cooks-Campbell, A. (2022, June 2). *What is mental strength? 7 ways to develop more than mental toughness.* Better Up. https://www.betterup.com/blog/mental-strength

Erb, K. P. (n.d.). *Willie Nelson, who saved his career and his house with the IRS tapes, turns 80.* Forbes. https://www.forbes.com/sites/kellyphillipserb/2013/04/29/willie-nelson-who-saved-his-career-and-his-house-with-the-irs-tapes-turns-80/?sh=bd8185855684

Gamma, E. (n.d.). *Brain Plasticity (Neuroplasticity)* Simply Psychology. https://www.simplypsychology.org/brain-plasticity.html#:~:text=Brain%20plasticity%2C%20also%20known%20as%20neuroplasticity%2C%20is%20the

Garvey, M. (2021, February 23). *Drew Barrymore talks about her experience in a "psychiatric ward" at 13.* CNN. https://www.cnn.com/2021/02/23/entertainment/drew-barrymore-psychiatric-ward-howard-stern/index.html#:~:text=Drew%20Barrymore%20was%20virtually%20interviewed%20on%20Howard%20Stern%E2%80%99s

Littlewood, Z. (2016, April 11). *Five Powerful Exercises to Improve Mental Toughness*. Mental Muscle Training. https://www.mentalmuscletraining.com/single-post/2016/04/10/5-POWERFUL-EXERCISES-TO-IMPROVE-MENTAL-TOUGHNESS

Mayo Clinic. (2018). *Fatigue Causes*. Mayo Clinic. https://www.mayoclinic.org/symptoms/fatigue/basics/causes/sym-20050894

Moore, C. (2019, January 14). *Resilience Training: How to master mental toughness and thrive.* PositivePsychology.com. https://positivepsychology.com/resilience-training/

Point of no return. (2022, March 24). Wikipedia. https://en.wikipedia.org/wiki/Point_of_no_return

Ranganathan, V. K., Siemionow, V., Liu, J. Z., Sahgal, V., & Yue, G. H. (2004). From mental power to muscle power--gaining strength by using the mind. *Neuropsychologia, 42*(7), 944–956. https://doi.org/10.1016/j.neuropsychologia.2003.11.018

Ribeiro, M. (2019, July 4). *How to Become Mentally Strong: 14 Strategies for Building Resilience*. Positive Psychology https://positivepsychology.com/mentally-strong/

The difference between Mental Health and Mental Strength. (2021, May 24). Hunimed. https://www.hunimed.eu/news/the-difference-between-mental-health-and-mental-strength/#:~:text=Mental%20health%20in%20most%20dictionaries

The Neuroscience of Perseverance. (n.d.). Psychology Today. https://www.psychologytoday.com/us/blog/the-athletes-way/201112/the-neuroscience-perseverance

Bergland, C. (2011, December 26). *The neuroscience of perseverance.* Psychology Today. https://www.psychologytoday.com/us/blog/the-athletes-way/201112/the-neuroscience-perseverance#:~:text=Dopamine%20is%20the%20fuel%20that%20keeps%20people%20motivated

Walt Disney's rocky road to success. (2020, June 17). Biography. https://www.biography.com/movies-tv/walt-disney-failures

Weingrad, E. (2015, October 27). *Drew Barrymore tells all to Howard in her Stern Show debut.* Howard Stern. https://www.howardstern.com/show/2015/10/27/drew-barrymore-tells-all-howard/

Why Mental Toughness Is Critically Important? (2020). Mental Toughness. https://www.mentaltoughness.partners/why-mental-toughness-is-critically-important/

Yousafzai, M. (n.d.). *Malala's story.* Malala. Malala.org. https://malala.org/malalas-story/

www.ingramcontent.com/pod-product-compliance
Lightning Source LLC
Chambersburg PA
CBHW061135120626
46546CB00005B/1798